THE MUGHAL EMPIRE

'In Brief': Books for Busy People

by Anne Davison

Copyright2017 Anne Davison

Books for Busy People

OTHER BOOKS BY THE SAME AUTHOR

Abraham's Children: Jew, Christian, Muslim; Commonality and Conflict

From the Medes to the Mullahs: a History of Iran

Making Sense of Militant Islam

Paul of Tarsus; a First Century Radical

The Holy Roman Empire: Power Politics Papacy

The Ottoman Empire

http://annedavison.org.uk

CONTENTS

PREFACE	4
INTRODUCTION	6
CHAPTER ONE: Out of Mongolia	9
CHAPTER TWO: Babur the Conqueror	20
CHAPTER THREE: Humayan in Exile	30
CHAPTER FOUR: Akbar the Great	39
CHAPTER FIVE: Jahangir, Conqueror of the World	51
CHAPTER SIX: Shah Jahan, King of the World	63
CHAPTER SEVEN: Aurangzeb the Austere	74
CHAPTER EIGHT: The Last Emperor	87
CONCLUSION	100
EPILOGUE	104
TIMELINE	106
WHO'S WHO AND WHAT'S WHAT	107
WORKS REFERRED TO	112

MAPS

Mongol Empire at the death of Genghis Khan, 1227	12
Successive Dynasties of Genghis Khan	14
Timurid Empire, 1370-1507	16
Genghis Khan Family Tree	20
Near Contemporaries of Babur	27
Mughal Empire at Death of Babur, 1530	29
Babur Family Tree	30
Mughal Empire under Akbar, 1605	43
Akbar Family Tree	53
Jahangir Family Tree	64
Mughal Empire under Aurangzeb, 1707	85

PREFACE

For some two hundred years, from the 16th Century to the 18th Century, a minority Islamic elite, the Mughals, ruled large swathes of Northern and Central India, which had a majority Hindu population. From the 18th Century onwards, the Mughal Empire went into decline, losing much of its power and territory to the Hindu Marathas and the British East India Company. When the last Emperor, Bahadur Shah II, came to the throne in 1837, Mughal power was confined to the city of Delhi and he was nothing more than a symbolic figurehead for the once powerful Empire. The British finally deposed Bahadur following the Indian Uprising in 1857. This marked the end of the Timurid Dynasty and the beginning of the British Raj.

The Mughal Emperors were enthusiastic patrons of the arts and literature. Most were accomplished calligraphers and poets. Two Emperors, Babur and Jahingir, wrote autobiographies. Under Mughal rule, magnificent monuments and mausoleums were commissioned, incorporating both Hindu and Islamic features in a unique Indo-Islamic style of architecture. Some of these monuments, for example the famous Taj Mahal and Humayan's tomb, are now popular tourist sites. Others, particularly in Delhi, were either destroyed during the Indian Uprising in 1857, or converted into military buildings by the British.

Much has been written about the final years of Mughal rule from a British perspective. This ranges from military accounts, British Government and East India Company documents as well as private diaries and letters, many of which are still hidden away in dusty archives.

More recently, primary source material has been made available to the public with the help of translations and digital technology. This material includes the biographies and autobiographies of the Emperors and also reports and accounts of European travellers, traders and missionaries.

The aim of this book is to provide an overview of this fascinating and complex history that should appeal to the non-academic. As with other books in the 'In Brief' series, this book is aimed at the general reader who wants to understand a particular historical topic but does not have the time or inclination to read a heavy academic tome. With this mind, footnotes have been omitted.

While there will inevitably be gaps in a book of this size, the intention is to cover the most significant events that moulded Mughal history. Should the reader be inspired to further reading on the subject, a small selection of the main works that have been consulted is provided at the end of the text.

Where possible maps and family trees are provided, which should help the reader follow the story. Furthermore, because the text contains so many names that may be unfamiliar, a 'Who's Who and What's What' is also provided.

Finally, I would like to thank those friends and colleagues who gave of their valuable time to read through various chapters, proof read the text, and offer helpful comments and advice.

INTRODUCTION

The word 'Mughal' is the Persian form of 'Mongol', reflecting the fact that the forerunners of the Mughal rulers of India were descendants of the Great Mongol, Genghis Khan. When Genghis died in 1227, his Empire was divided among his four sons, a practice that was continued by his descendants across Central Asia. One branch of the Mongol dynasty eventually came under the rule of Timur, also known as Tamerlane (Timur the Lame). Timur founded the Timurid Empire (1370-1507) that stretched from today's Turkey in the West to Pakistan in the East.

In 1483, Zahir-ud-Din Muhammad, known as Babur, was born into the House of Timur at Mawarannahr, modern Uzbekistan. On the death of his father, Babur inherited the region of Fergana Valley but he lost his land to other male relatives. Believing he had no prospects in his homeland he decided to travel eastwards into Hindustan where, in 1526, he conquered the Sultanate of Delhi. Babur then became the first Mughal Emperor of India, a dynasty that was referred to as the House of Timur.

The Mughal Empire enjoyed its greatest period of expansion, power, cultural flowering and religious tolerance, during the rule of Akbar the Great (1556-1605). Following the death of the sixth Emperor Aurangzeb, in 1707, the Empire went into steady decline and was finally dissolved in 1857 in the aftermath of the Indian Uprising, or Mutiny.

The reasons for the decline of the Empire were multiple. In 1738, the Persians under Nadir Shah attacked Delhi from the West while the Hindu Maratha Empire persistently pushed into Mughal territory from the South East. However, the greatest challenge to the Mughals came from the growing presence and influence of Europeans.

The British, Dutch and Portuguese first arrived on the Indian sub-continent as traders during the 15th and 16th Centuries. By the 17th Century the English East India Company was well established in Calcutta and Madras. In the early years of the Company's existence, relations between the Indian population and the British were good, with many British men marrying Hindu and Muslim women and adopting an Indian lifestyle. However, in the 18th Century, with the rise of the Christian Evangelical movement in England, attitudes changed. From this point onwards the British increasingly advocated conversion of the native 'heathen' to Christianity. Hinduism in particular was portrayed as an 'evil, debauched religion'.

By the middle of the 19th Century, relations between the British officers of the East India Company and the native sepoy army completely broke down. In May 1857, Indian troops across Northern India turned against their British commanders in what became known as the Indian Uprising or Indian Mutiny.

After several months of vicious fighting and atrocities committed by both sides, the British finally put down the rebellion. The Emperor was arrested and the Mughal Empire was dissolved. The East India Company and its territories subsequently formed part of the British Empire and Queen Victoria became Empress of India.

The first Chapter traces the history of the Mongols under the leadership of Genghis Khan and Timur. If the reader is not particularly interested in Mongol history, the story of the Mughal Empire can be picked up in Chapter Two. However, since the Turkic Mongol inheritance is so important to Mughal identity, the background that is provided in Chapter One provides useful reading.

Chapters two to seven cover the rule of the first six Emperors, from Babur to Aurangzeb. This is considered to be the greatest period of Mughal history. The final chapter tells of the Empire's slow decline, until the Emperor's role was purely symbolic, with the real power being in the hands of the British.

The history of a region that covers several centuries presents a problem with boundaries, which can change and be porous. Place names can also be confusing. For example, Persia is also referred to as Iran and the boundary between Persia, India and

Afghanistan frequently changed. Furthermore, the spelling of names can vary. For example, Amir can also be spelt Emir and Ferghana as Fergana or Farghana. Where possible, the spelling that might be more familiar to a Western reader, has been used throughout the text.

In the 16th Century, the region that Babur conquered was known as Hindustan, which was the Persian name for India. The region of Bengal that is referred to in the text is now known as Bangladesh. Madras is now known as Chennai and Bombay as Mumbai.

CHAPTER ONE

Out of Mongolia

Genghis Khan

The story of the Mughal Empire can be traced back to the life of Genghis Khan, sometimes referred to as the 'Great Khan' or 'Universal Ruler', who founded the Mongol Empire in 1206. Most of what is known about Genghis is taken from the *Secret History of the Mongols,* which is the oldest surviving literary work in the Mongolian language. It was written in 1227 by an anonymous author after the death of the Great Khan and tells the story of his life, his rise to power and creation of an empire that eventually stretched from the Black Sea in the West to the Eastern coast of China.

Genghis was born Temujin, Temu meaning 'iron', around 1162 in the mountainous area of Burkhan Khaldun in today's northern Mongolia. He was the second son of Yesugei who was chief of the Borigin clan and he was the first son of Hoelun, his father's chief wife. He was therefore considered to be of minor noble birth. It is said that the child was born with a clot of blood clenched in his hand which was traditionally considered by the Mongols to be a favourable sign, signifying that he would grow up to be a great leader. However, it is likely that this embellishment to his birth narrative was added after his death.

At that time, there were numerous tribes and clans spread across the steppe lands of today's Mongolia, China and into the Gobi Desert. The tribes were grouped into loose confederations such as the Mongols, Tatars, Merkits, and Naimans. They were nomadic and competed for grazing pastures, a situation that led to tribal raids and inter-clan warfare. In order to survive they formed friendly alliances that were often sealed through inter-clan marriage and it was not unusual for a clan chief to steal a wife from another tribe in order to cement an alliance. In fact, this is what happened in the case of Temujin's parents. Yesugei snatched Hoelun from the chief of the neighbouring Merkit tribe, just as she was about to become the chief's bride. Since a clan's wealth was judged by its size, the theft of horses, women and children, all of which were highly prized, was a quick and useful way to enlarge the clan.

In accordance with Mongol tradition, Yesugei arranged a marriage between his nine-year old son Temujin and Borte of the Khongirad tribe with the aim of cementing a friendly alliance. As a sign of good faith in the alliance, Temujin was sent to live with Borte's family until they were of marriageable age, which was usually between 12 and 15 years.

When Temujin was about 15 years he received the news that the Tatars, traditional enemies of the Borijin, had killed his father by poisoning. He therefore decided to go back to his tribe and take over Yesugei's role as head of the clan. But he was not made welcome by the other male relatives and his claim to headship was rejected. His widowed mother Hoelun, and all her children were cast out leaving them with no clan protection. A few centuries later Babur, a descendent of Temujin and the first Mughal Emperor, was to suffer the same experience.

Being without a clan the small group of refugees, which included his brothers and half-brothers, were forced to wander the steppe in poverty, surviving on wild fruits and small hunted game.

There were inevitable tensions between the brothers, which finally erupted when Temujin's eldest half-brother Begter, claimed the right to take Hoelun as his wife. Under Mongol law, since Hoelun was not the mother of Begter, he was within his rights. But this angered Temujin. A fight broke out and Temujin, with the help of his full brother Khasar, killed Begter.

Sometime after this a rival clan captured Temujin. He was imprisoned in a cangue, which is a type of portable wooden stocks, but eventually, with the help of a friendly guard, he managed to escape. He was now free to marry Borte but soon after the wedding she was captured by the Merkits. This could have been a tit for tat act in revenge for Yesugie's earlier theft of his mother Hoelen from the Merkits.

Temujin turned to his friend Jamukha and also to the Toghrul

Khan of the Keraite tribe for help and between them they were able to rescue Borte. About nine months later Borte gave birth to a son Jochi. This naturally led to speculation that Temujin may not be the father of the child. As a result, Jochi was never accepted as the natural successor to his father. Borte went on to have three more sons: Chagatai, Ogedei and Tolui. Temujin fathered numerous other children with further wives and concubines but his sons with Borte remained in senior position and his direct heirs.

Having secured the support of Toghrul, Khan of the Keraites, Temujin went on to consolidate his power by forming alliances with all other clans within the Mongol confederacy. In 1186, he was elected Khan of the Mongols. By 1206 he went further by bringing the Merkits, Naimans, Tatars, Uyghurs and numerous other smaller groups within his orbit of power. This united group of tribes became known collectively as the Mongols and Temujin acquired the title Genghis Khan. At the time of his death in 1227 his Empire stretched from the Caspian Sea, incorporating the Kwarezmian Empire, to the border of today's Korea including the Chinese Jin Dynasty.

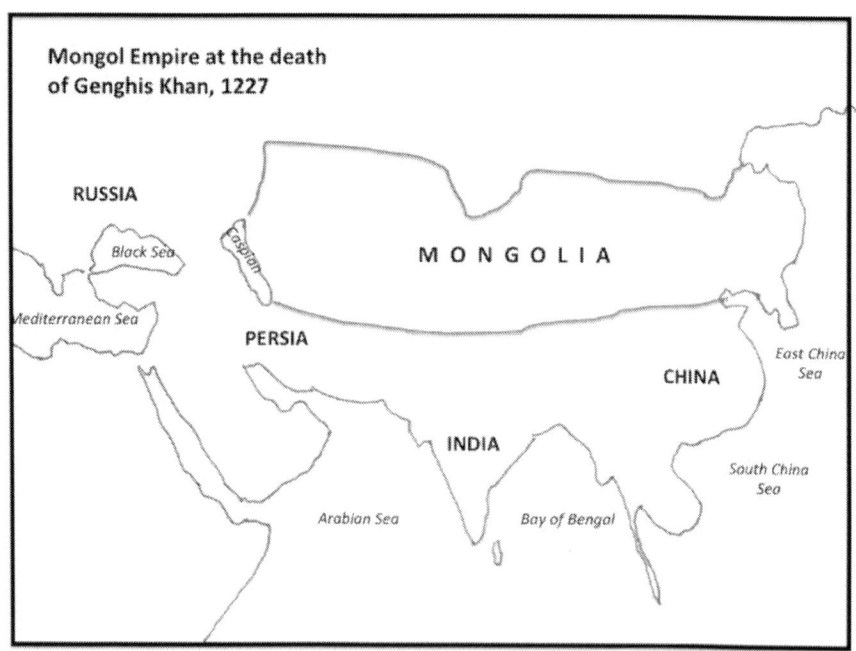

Genghis Khan was clearly a brilliant, though brutal, military leader. He was also a clever strategist. His new Empire stretched across the ancient Silk Route bringing him a new source of great wealth. But this had only been possible because the Great Khan had first been able to unite the Mongol tribes around a common cause instead of fighting each other.

From an early age Temujin understood the importance of acquiring strong alliances, something that had been instilled in him by his mother Hoelun. Only through forging alliances could the Mongols hope to gain and maintain power. He also knew that the alternative, clan warfare, led to instability and suffering, both of which he had experienced as a youth.

His policy therefore was to cement alliances wherever possible, often through inter-clan marriages. In order to further break down tribal loyalty he put men from different clans together rather than have units made up of the same clan or tribe. In this way he weakened clan and tribe loyalty while at the same time unifying and strengthening loyalty to his central army.

As was the practice with all Turkic tribes, he invited defeated cities to surrender and pay tribute. If they refused, he would either kill the men or take them into his armies to use as human shields. By removing the men, he removed the possibility of future rebellion and by capturing them he acquired a useful military tool in the form of cannon fodder.

The elderly would have been of no use and were therefore killed. Younger women and children were valuable and so taken as slaves. Many women were given as wives to his men and often the healthiest children were brought up alongside Mongol children as part of the family, thereby increasing the Mongol population.

Genghis Khan increased the wealth of his Empire by taking everything of value from conquered cities. He also captured everyone who was skilled in engineering, military tactics and administration. In this way, he acquired the expertise that he needed in order to consolidate and expand. Since he had no experience in siege warfare he particularly needed that aspect of military expertise.

Two other features of leadership marked Genghis Khan's rule. First, he appointed his generals according to meritocracy rather than on a hereditary basis and secondly, he valued loyalty above all else, even if that loyalty was to the detriment of his own position.

Genghis Khan died in 1227 at the age of 62. Because of doubts over the paternity of Jochi, his eldest son, and the instability of his second son Chagatai, Genghis decided before his death to divide the Empire between his four sons, with the succession as Great Khan passing to his third son Ogedei.

Jochi was given the Western part of the Empire that included the region of the Caucasus and parts of today's Russia. His sons were to found the Golden Horde that ruled the region from 1240 until 1502 when it then broke up into smaller khanates. Chagatai received Central Asia and Northern Iran. Ogedei received Eastern Asia and China while the youngest son, Tolui, was given the Mongol homeland, roughly equating to present day Mongolia.

In relation to Mughal history, which is the topic of this book, we are interested in Chagatai's inheritance of Central Asia and Northern Iran, which eventually fell to the Timurids.

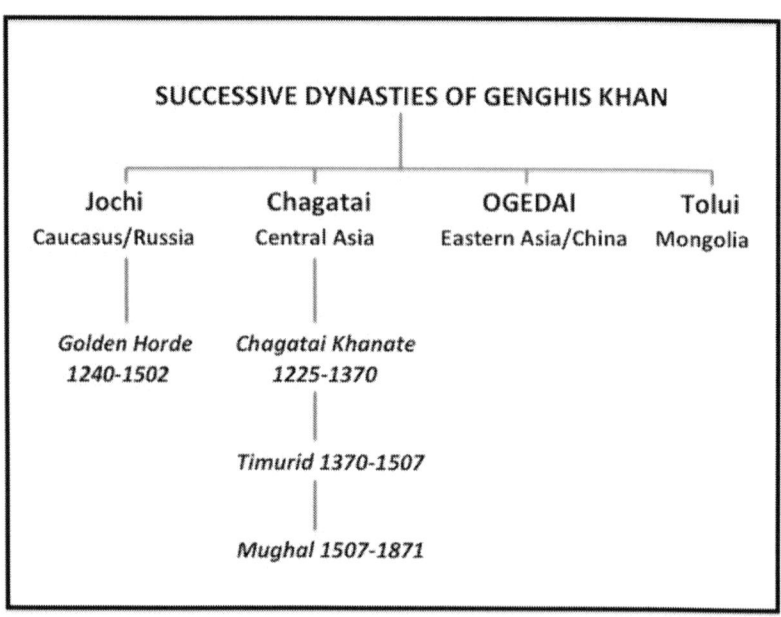

Timur

If the name of Genghis Khan struck fear into the hearts of those he conquered, then equally, if not more so, did Timur. He was also known as Timur the Lame on account of his disability, whic then became Tamerlane or Tamberlaine in the West.

In 1336, just over a hundred years after the death of Genghis Khan, Timur was born near Samarkand in today's Uzbekistan. In common with many children of the steppe, he was taken captive by a Mongol tribe at the age of about nine, together with his mother and brothers. From an early age, he began raiding travelers and stealing sheep, cattle and horses. It is believed that on one of these raids he was shot in the leg and arm by two arrows that left him crippled for life, hence the name Timur the Lame.

At that time, Samarkand was part of the Chagatai Khanate. Timur was born into the Barlas tribe that was ethnically Mongol but had been Turkified, possibly by the Seljuk Turks who had swept across Eastern and Central Asia towards Anatolia in the 10th Century.

Although Timur had been born into the region of the Chagatai Khanate, which had been founded by Genghis Khan's son Chagatai, he was unable to claim direct descent from the Great Khan because he was a member of the Barlas tribe rather than Genghis's own tribe, the Borijin. By marrying Saray Mulk Khanum, a princess of the Chagatai Khanate and direct descendant of Genghis Khan, Timur legitimised his claim to be the rightful successor to Genghis. He therefore believed that he should continue the work of Genghis and restore, unify and expand the Mongol Empire.

Unlike Genghis Khan, who followed Tengrism, a Central Asian religion that features shamanism, animism and ancestor worship, Timur was born a Muslim into the Naqshbandi Sufi tradition. Most Naqshbandis trace their lineage to Ali and the Shi'a branch of Islam. However, Timur followed a pragmatic path and was prepared to treat Shi'a Muslims just as harshly as anyone else if it suited his purpose.

He styled himself 'The Sword of Islam' and *Ghazi* (Muslim warrior) and used Islamic symbols and rhetoric to urge his armies on when on campaign. In the process he converted many of those he conquered, for example Genghis Khan's Borijin tribe, to Islam.

From his base in the Chagatai Khanate, Timur conquered Central, Southern and Western Asia, the Caucasus and Russia. Further west he beat the Mamluks who at that time ruled Egypt and Syria. He also seized territory from the nascent Ottoman Empire in Anatolia and from the Sultanate of Delhi in India. In 1370, he became the first ruler of the vast Timurid Empire that was to last until 1507 when parts of the Eastern region succumbed to the MughalEmpire.

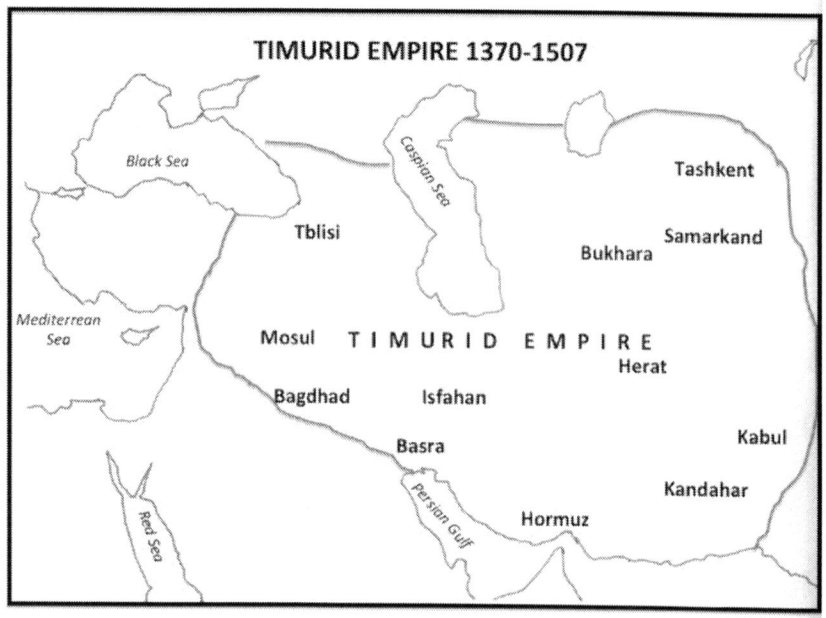

In contrast to Genghis, who remained a nomad throughout his life and showed little interest in settling, Timur founded and fortified great cities such as Samarkand, which became his capital. He commissioned Islamic schools and appointed governors to run towns and cities. He also encouraged his followers to intermarry and settle in conquered lands as had Alexander the Great some fifteen hundred years earlier.

Much of the area that he came to rule was Persian and gradually there developed a synthesis of Persian and Turkic culture. Timur himself became proficient in Persian, Mongolian and Turkic languages. He was a patron of the arts and literature and during his reign he commissioned magnificent monuments that became known as the Timurid style of architecture.

While Timur's cultural legacy was positive, he is better known in the West for his brutality. He imposed crippling taxes on his subject peoples. His punishments were always public with the aim of instilling fear in the populace rather than punishment for a crime. This tactic was normal in medieval Europe with its public executions such as hanging, drawing and quartering and more recently *Daesh* have followed the same policy with public beheadings. In Timur's case he regularly built pyramids of enemy skulls or cemented them into walls for all to see. A common statistic given for the number of deaths at the hands of Timur is 17 million, representing about 5% of the world's population at the time.

He is particularly remembered for the capture of Beyizid I, the Ottoman Sultan known as the 'Thunderbolt' on account of his rapid marches across Anatolia. Beyizid was captured by Timur in July 1402 at the Battle of Ankara and died in captivity the following year. In December 1402, Timur laid siege to Smyna on the coast of Anatolia, which at that time was in the hands of the Christian Knights Hospitaller, also known as the Knights of St John. Timur offered the 200 knights safe protection in return for a heavy tribute. When this was refused, he carried out his traditional act of massacre and destruction.

Two years later, while preparing for a campaign into China, Timur was taken ill. Just before his death in February 1405, he designated his grandson Pir Muhammad ibn Jahangir as his successor. The succession was contested by other male claimants and, as so often happened, there followed a period of some fifteen years infighting and instability.

By 1467, the Timurids had lost much of their Persian territory to the Ag Qoyunlu, a Sunni tribal federation that was also known as the White Sheep Turkomans. The White Sheep had ruled an area including present-day Azerbaijan, Armenia, Eastern Turkey and parts of Iran and Iraq between 1378 and 1501. In 1501, Shah Ismail I founded the Shi'a Safavid Dynasty in Persia securing even more Timurid land and between 1505 and 1507 the Uzbeks conquered the Timurid capital of Samarkand and also Herat.

Although by 1507 the Timurid Empire had collapsed, the dynasty survived in the form of separate Timurid emirates. A Timurid prince named Babur founded one such emirate in Kabul, modern Afghanistan. He was later to found the Mughal Empire.

Conclusion

Genghis Khan was the second son of the chief of the Borijin clan that was one of the many clans that made up the Mongol federation. At the time of his birth in the 12th Century, numerous nomadic tribes competed for pastures and control of the lucrative Silk Route. This led to inter-clan warfare and great instability. Only the sealing of alliances could bring a measure of peace.

Genghis Khan's genius was that he not only recognised the need for peace between the clans but that he was also able to seal valuable alliances. This ability put him on the path to power. It was not unusual at that time for alliances to be broken and clan chiefs to swap sides. Consequently, Genghis placed great emphasis on loyalty. In an effort to break down clan loyalty in favour of loyalty to himself as rightful leader of all Mongols, he formed multi-clan fighting units. He also appointed his generals on merit rather than the traditional hereditary system. This further strengthened the central army.

Throughout his lifetime, Genghis Khan remained a nomad and follower of the Central Asian religion of Tengrism. When he died in 1227 his vast empire was divided between his four sons. His third son, Ogedei, succeeded as Great Khan and was given Eastern Asia and China. Jochi, the eldest son received the Western Region including the Caucasus and his sons later founded the Golden Horde.

Chagatai, the second son received Central Asia and Iran, which by this time was Muslim. Consequently, when Timur was born in 1336 near Samarkand in the Chagatai Khanate, he was born a Muslim and he styled himself 'The Sword of Islam'. Through his marriage to a Borigin princess, Timur claimed direct descent from Genghis Khan and legitimised his aggressive territorial campaigns on the grounds that it was his duty to restore and reunite the Mongol Empire. He also believed that it was his Islamic duty to conquer the infidel.

In contrast to Genghis Khan, Timur founded great cities and patronised art and culture. Some wonderful examples of Timurid architecture and works of art can still be found in Central Asia and in museums around the world.

From a Western perspective both Genghis Khan and Timur, or Tamerlane, have been portrayed as perhaps the most brutal conquerors in history. But in Central and Eastern Asian countries they are viewed as heroes. Indeed, since the fall of communism in the region, both have enjoyed a renaissance. An example would be the impressive Amir Timur Square in Tashkent, Uzbekistan, which commemorates the life of Timur and has become both a place of pilgrimage and a popular tourist attraction.

Prince Babur, who was to found the Mughal Empire, was a direct descendent of both Genghis Khan and Timur. He was a Timurid and when he invaded Hindustan in 1526 he took with him a Turkic-Mongol heritage and a Timurid dynasty.

CHAPTER TWO

Babur the Conqueror

The Early Years

Babur, which means 'tiger' in Persian, was born on the 14th February 1483 in Andijan, which is a city in the Ferghana Valley of Uzbekistan. At that time, it was part of the Timurid Empire. He was the eldest son of Umar Sheikh Mirza who was the Amir, or ruler, of Ferghana. He was also a direct descendant of Timur on his father's side and Genghis Khan on his mother's side.

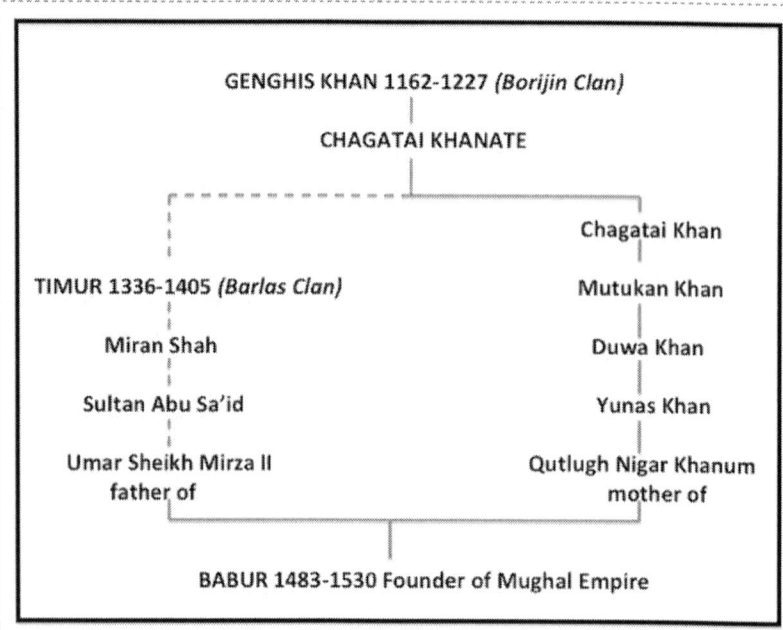

When Babur was about 12 years old his father died following a fall from a dovecote that was attached to the side of the palace. The young Babur then became the rightful successor as Amir of Ferghana. However, as is often the case when a minor inherits a kingdom, other male relatives were quick to challenge his accession.

We get most of our information about the life of Babur from his own autobiography, known as the *Baburnama*, meaning the 'Book' or 'Letters of Babur'. The book was written in the Chagatai language of the Andijan-Timurids and was later translated, during the reign of Akbar the Great, into Persian. It contains not just details about Babur's many military campaigns but also his reflections on Hindustan, together with illustrations of the fauna, flora and people of the region. The autobiography reveals him to be a competent and ambitious military leader but also a man of deep sensitivity and creativity.

Babur begins the *Baburnama* with the words:

'In the month of Ramadan of the year 899 and in the twelfth year of my age, I became ruler in the country of Farghana.'

But Babur's accession was not to go smoothly. Ever since the death of Timur, the succeeding princes had fought among themselves over territory. Ferghana was just one of the many small kingdoms ruled by a Timurid prince and once news of the death its Amir spread, the neighbouring chiefs, who were all related to Babur, caste covetous eyes on his Kingdom.

The Kingdom of Ferghana was set in a valley providing pasture for sheep, goats and the famous short-legged Mongol horse, which was probably the most valuable possession of the nomadic people. Measuring approximately two hundred miles long and a hundred miles wide, Ferghana had no important cities and therefore was not a particularly wealthy region. Despite this, Babur's uncles and cousins formed an alliance with the intention of ousting the young ruler.

It was his maternal grandmother Aisan Daulat Begum, a direct descendant of Genghis Khan, who became his greatest support when he was most vulnerable. From early childhood Babur, along with other young Timurids, had instilled in him the significance of his bloodline; that he carried in his veins the blood not only of Timur the Conqueror but also the Great Khan Genghis. His grandmother encouraged him to stand firm as was befitting his bloodline and defend his inheritance.

For the next seven years, he was in constant warfare with his relatives. During this time, he twice lost Ferghana but he succeeded, at the age of 15, in taking the Timurid capital of

Samarkand, only to lose it again just 100 days later. By 1501 he had not only lost Samarkand to the Uzbeks but he had also lost his home of Ferghana to his relatives. He spent the next few years wandering the mountains of Central Asia with a small band of followers. Throughout this time, he had the support of his grandmother and at one point he was given refuge in Tashkent with a maternal uncle. While in Tashkent, Babur decided to concentrate on building up his army.

In 1504, some ten years after becoming ruler of Ferghana, Babur decided to give up the fight for his ancestral homeland and look elsewhere. An opportunity came when the ruler of Kabul, from the Arghun Dynasty, suddenly died leaving an infant son as his only heir. In the usual steppe tradition neighbouring princes, including Babur, were quick to stake a claim. This time Babur was successful. The Arghuns were forced to retreat to Kandahar and Babur took the city of Kabul where he remained ruler until 1526.

Years in Kabul

Babur's years in Kabul were relatively peaceful. By this time, he had proven himself as a respected leader and the threat from other Timurid princes declined. The only real danger to his position came from the Uzbeks.

Soon after taking Kabul, realising that the city would never generate much wealth, he made his first raid through the Khyber Pass into Hindustan. At this point his aim was not to conquer but to make a quick raid, seize what he could, and return with his booty.

He also spent some time in Herat, which was a highly-cultured city at the time. Here he met the poet Mir Ali Shir Nava'i who has been credited with developing the Chagatai language and is thought to have influenced Babur in his decision to use Chagatai for his autobiography, the *Baburnama*.

During his time in Kabul, Babur developed good relations with the two main Islamic Empires in the region. First, he forged an alliance with the Safavid Shah Ismail I of Persia so that together they could fight off the Uzbeks. Secondly, his relationship with the Ottomans strengthened when the Sultan offered to provide Babur with artillery expertise and munitions such as cannons and matchlock rifles. This military hardware was to give him a huge advantage when he later invaded Hindustan.

While in Kabul, Babur put down numerous rebellions and gradually the remaining Timurid princes and chieftains looked to him for protection against their enemies and particularly against the Uzbeks. As a result, Babur assumed the title Padshah (King) among the Timurids. Although by this time large swathes of the Timurid Empire had been lost to the Ottomans, Safavids or Uzbeks, the title of Padshah was symbolically important and augured well for Babur's future.

Into Hindustan

Although Babur was now King of Kabul and Padshah of the Timurids, he was still under constant threat from the Uzbeks. He therefore decided to give up the idea of establishing a kingdom in his homelands and to try his luck to the East, in Hindustan. In 1519, he crossed the Khyber Pass into the Punjab. His intention was to establish a new Kingdom that would be safe from invading Uzbeks. Another attraction was the great wealth to be found in the cities of Lahore and Delhi. Furthermore, by conquering the region of modern Pakistan he would be restoring territory that was previously part of the Timurid Empire.

The region of Northern India was at that time ruled by the Delhi Sultanate, a Muslim kingdom that had been in power under various dynasties since 1206. The Sultanate was more a federation of states rather than a unified entity. From 1517, Ibrahim, an Ethnic Afghan of the Afghan Lodi Dynasty, ruled as Sultan. He was an incapable and unpopular ruler and during his reign there were many defections from his amirs and clan leaders. One small group, led by the Governor of the Punjab, Dawlat Khan Lodi, invited Babur to attack Delhi and overthrow Ibrahim.

Babur accepted the invitation, seeing it as a way to establish himself in Hindustan. By November 1525, he had conquered the

Punjab. In April 1526, his armies had reached Panipat in Northern India. On the 21st April Babur's forces engaged with the armies of Ibrahim Lodi at the First Battle of Panipat, said to be the first battle in India to use gunpowder firearms and field artillery.

Statistics vary from 50,000 to 100,000 troops, plus about 100 war elephants, in Ibrahim's force. Babur's armies were thought to be far less, at around 12,000 men, but he had the great advantage of firearms and cannon. He also utilised war tactics learned from the Ottomans. The result of the battle was a resounding victory for Babur, who suffered few losses. On the other hand, Ibrahim died in battle, together with some 6,000 of his men. Many of the Lodi casualties were the result of being trampled upon by terrified elephants that went berserk at the sound of the cannon.

The Battle marked the end of the Lodi Dynasty and the founding of the Mughal Empire in India. Babur recorded the event in his memoirs with the following words:

'By the grace of the Almighty God, this difficult task was made easy to me and that mighty army, in the space of a half a day, was laid in dust.'

Among the booty seized by Babur following the Battle of Panipat was the famous Koh-i-Noor diamond. It is thought that the stone originally came from one of the many mines in today's Andhra Pradesh that were famous at the time for emeralds, rubies and especially diamonds. By the 14th Century, the Koh-i-Noor diamond was in the hands of the Khalji dynasty of the Delhi Sultanate. Following the Battle of Panipat, the diamond remained with the Mughal emperors until 1739, when the Persian Nadir Shah seized it when he invaded Delhi. It then changed hands several times until it came into the possession of the British in 1849 and from that time it has been part of the British Crown Jewels.

In March 1527, just a year after defeating Ibrahim Lodi, Babur faced a challenge from Rana Sanga, the Rajput Hindu ruler of Mewar. Sanga had expected Babur to return to Afghanistan with his loot after the Battle of Panipat, as Timur and other Timurids had in previous decades. When Babur showed signs of staying in Delhi and laying the foundations of a Mughal Kingdom, Sanga formed an alliance of disaffected Afghan chiefs with the aim of ousting the Timurid usurper.

When Babur discovered that the Rajput-Afghan coalition had rallied many more troops than his own forces, he decided that the seriousness of the situation called for drastic action. First, he gave up all alcohol, vowing never to drink it again. Whether he saw this as an act of penitence, since Muslims are officially forbidden alcohol, or whether his decision was one of pragmatism to ensure a clear mind, is not known.

Secondly, he appealed to all Afghans in the enemy forces to come over to his side on the grounds of religion. He claimed that all Muslims should unite against the Hindu infidel. In other words, he called a *Jihad* against the Rajputs and referred to himself as *Ghazi* (Muslim warrior).

On the 16th March 1527, the two forces met at the Battle of Khanwa, which is a small village East of Agra. Once more, despite Babur's weakness in numbers, he defeated Rana Sanga largely on account of superior munitions and also the fact that a faction of Sanga's army changed sides and joined Babur. Furthermore, by this time Babur was an experienced leader and military strategist and this no doubt added to his success over the less experienced Hindus. Rana Sanga managed to escape the battlefield but his alliance fell apart.

With the Battle of Khanwa, Babur consolidated his power in Hindustan. As a warning to others who may think to challenge his rule, he ordered that the skulls of the defeated be built into a tower, as had been the practice of his ancestor Timur.

Babur was 43 years old when he began to lay the foundations of the Mughal Empire. Until this time, he had spent all his life in Central Asia. As an ethnic Turco-Mongol and a direct descendent of Timur and Genghis Khan he had inherited the nomadic tradition of the steppe people. He was most at home on horseback, hunting in the mountains or riding out on campaign.

The land he now ruled was quite different. He found it too hot in the summer and not totally to his liking. According to the *Baburnama* he records:

"*Hindustan is a country of few charms and the people do not have good looks. The people had no genius, no comprehension of mind, no politeness of manner.*"

His solution to his sense of alienation was to introduce elements from his own Central Asian culture, that in turn was greatly influenced by Persian culture. He planted gardens in the Persian style with fountains and running water. He imported plants, flowers and fruits. His memoirs also speak of his admiration for the fauna and flora that was native to Hindustan, indicating that he recognised beauty where he saw it.

He also commissioned the building of monuments and mosques. One mosque of significance, that was built during Babur's time, was the *Babri Masjid* meaning Babur's Mosque. It was built at Ayodhya in Uttar Pradesh on the site of a Hindu temple that some Hindus claim marked the birthplace of the Hindu deity Lord Rama. In 1992, a group of Hindu extremists, who wanted to reclaim the site and build a Hindu temple, destroyed the mosque. This sparked an interreligious dispute that erupted into violence resulting in around 2,000 deaths. In 2011, the Supreme Court of India decreed that the site should be divided between the contesting parties.

Following his conquest of Delhi, Babur only enjoyed four years as Mughal Emperor. He died in December 1530 and was buried at his beloved Kabul. Although Babur had been a successful leader and ruler, he had been less successful in his personal life. He had shown little interest in women and marriage as a young man, preferring the company of male friends. While this was normal in the steppe culture of the time, Babur was particularly reluctant to marry and spent most of his leisure time with a young soldier named Baburi.

His first marriage to his paternal cousin Aisha Sultan Begun was unsuccessful and produced no heir. He later married several times and had many children. His first son, Humayan, was the product of his marriage to his fourth wife Maham Begum. On Babur's death in 1530, Humayan succeeded to the throne and became the second Mughal Emperor.

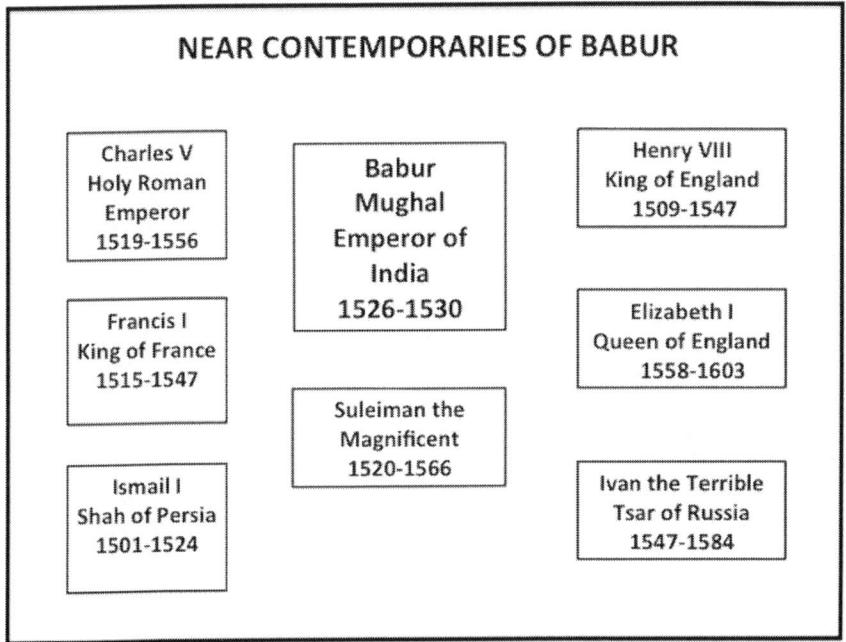

Conclusion

Babur's success in conquering Delhi and founding the Mughal Empire was mainly due to his skills as an experienced military leader and a shrewd political strategist.

As a young boy growing up in the hostile steppe county of Central Asia, he was quick to learn, and came to love the riding and hunting skills necessary for survival. His first real test in life came with the death of his father when he was just 12 years old. Although at that time he had lost his rightful inheritance, with the support of his grandmother, he displayed a determination to never give up. This was a trait that stayed with him for life and it was based on his strong sense of destiny.

As a Timurid prince he believed it was is duty to follow in the footsteps of the great Timur. When he succeeded, at just 15 years old, in taking the wealthy and cultured city of Samarkand, which was the capital city of Timur, this further convinced him of his destiny.

From his autobiography, the *Baburnama*, Babur often appears to be a man of sensitivity and appreciative of ascetic beauty. However, on the battlefield he could be as ruthless as his forebear Timur. In tribal society, where changes of alliance were commonplace, he knew the importance of gaining and maintaining loyalty. He did this both by instilling fear and also offering reward where it was due. In other words, he used the 'carrot and stick' method.

For all the military skills displayed by Babur, his success was also due to his ability to take advantage of the enemy's weakness. This was particularly the case when he succeeded in taking Kabul and even more so with Delhi. In Kabul, he used the age-old strategy of striking at a time when the heir to the throne was a minor, indeed, an infant. With Delhi, he accepted an invitation from Afghan chieftains, who were subject to the Lodi dynasty, to overthrow their unpopular ruler Ibrahim Lodi.

Consequently, in just four years, the 43 years old Babur succeeded in founding a Timurid Dynasty in Hindustan, to be known as the Mughal Empire. From its capital at Delhi, a Turkic-Mongol Muslim elite would rule a majority Hindu population for the next two hundred years.

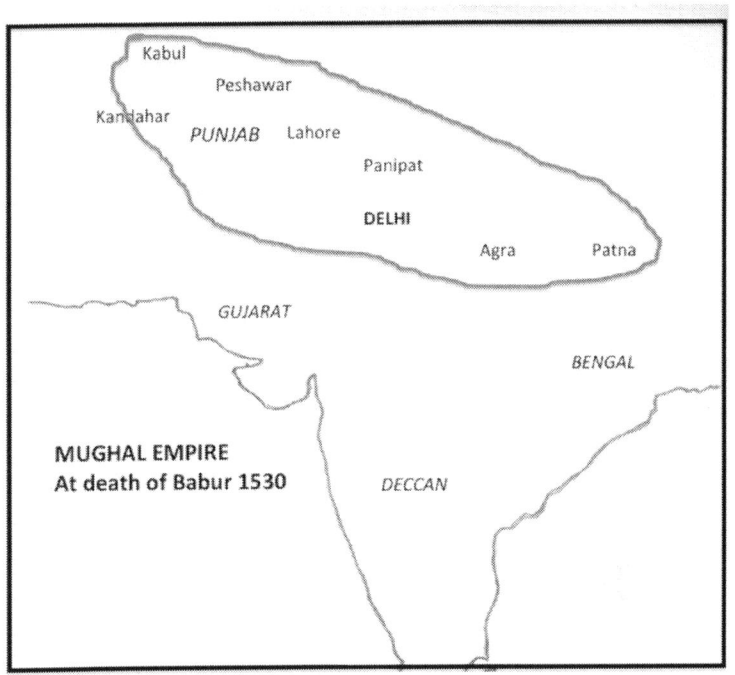

CHAPTER THREE

Humayan and Exile

A Fragile Beginning

Before Babur died in 1530 he decided, in the Central Asian tradition of Genghis Khan, to divide his Empire between his two eldest sons. Humayan, the elder of the two inherited the title Emperor of the Mughal Empire with his capital initially at Agra. His half-brother, Kamran Mirza, became ruler of the Punjab, which included the cities of Kabul and Lahore. Whereas the division of the Mongol Empire at the death of Genghis Khan was relatively successful, this was not normally the case. The more common situation was that siblings competed for the throne leading to open conflict and often fratricide.

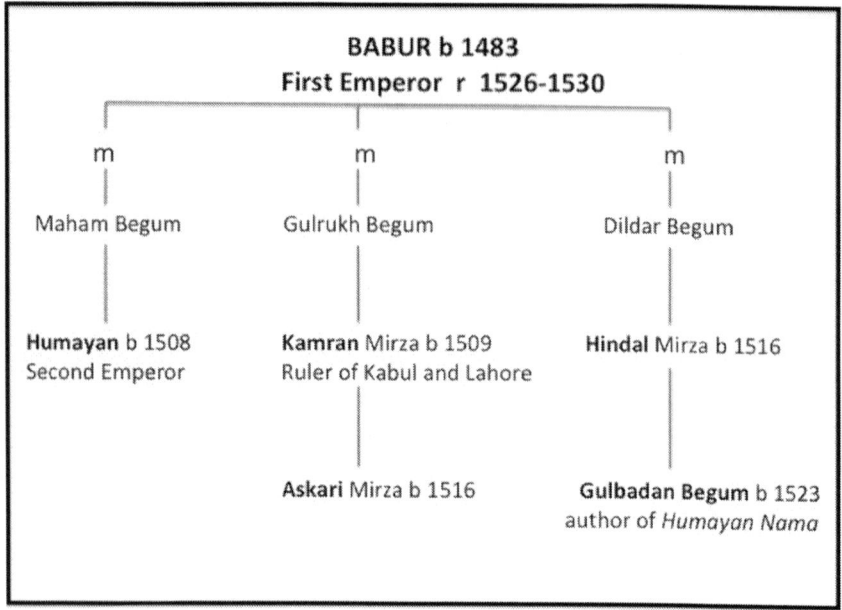

We get most of our information about the life of Humayan from the biography of his life, the *Humayun Nama* that was written by his sister Gulbadan Begum. Akbar, Humayan's son and successor, commissioned the work and an incomplete copy of the manuscript is currently held in the British Museum. It was discovered and sold to the British Library in the 1860s and was translated into English in 1902 by Annette Beveridge.

Humayan inherited an Empire that had only been existence for four years and consequently it was extremely fragile. Although Babur defeated Ibrahim Lodi, the previous ruler of Delhi, at the Battle of Panipat, he had not destroyed the Lodi dynasty, which remained a threat to Humayan's rule. Humayan also faced a challenge from other Afghan nobles in the region. Furthermore, he soon discovered that he could not rely on any support from his brothers or other male relatives.

Babur, the first Emperor, had experienced hardship and homelessness. In battle, he suffered many disappointments and defeat before finally succeeding in establishing his kingdom. Humayan, on the other hand, enjoyed an education befitting a prince. He was proficient in several languages, plus mathematics, philosophy and astrology. But he was more interested in Persian art and culture than diplomacy and the art of war. Although Humayan had played a significant part in the Battles of Panipat and Khanwa against the Lodi dynasty, he was still relatively inexperienced in military affairs. Therefore, in order to prepare him for his future role, his father appointed him, at the age of 20, as Governor of Badakhashan, an area North of Kabul.

When Humayan came to the throne in 1530, the Mughal presence was little more than a military occupation. Furthermore, since the cities of Kabul and Kandahar were no longer in his possession, he was deprived of a valuable source of recruitment. In this vulnerable situation, he also faced two major threats, both of which were from other Muslim powers. The first was from Sultan Bahadur of Gujarat to the Southwest and the second from the Afghan leader Sher Shah Suri (Sher Khan) of Bihar to the East. Humayan found himself in a difficult situation because he did not have the resources to send troops to both regions at the same time. If he concentrated on Bihar he was open to attack from Bahadur of Gujarat and equally if he challenged Bahadur he was unable to defend himself from Sher Khan.

Humayan's first campaign was aimed at subduing Sher Khan in the East but he was forced to return to Delhi when the city came under attack from Bahadur. This was a pattern that was to continue for much of his early reign.

The situation was further complicated by the presence of the Portuguese, the first European power to establish trading posts on the Indian Subcontinent. The Portuguese were particularly interested in the coastal region of Gujarat, which brought them into conflict with Sultan Bahadur. In exchange for trade concessions with the Portuguese, Bahadur received firearms and military help. This presented a serious threat to Humayan who, until that time, had been the only power in the region with firearms, which had given him an advantage over his enemies. Now Bahadur, with his Portuguese munitions, was on an equal footing.

Unlike his father, Humayan did not possess the diplomatic and military skills to deal with the situation. Nor did he have the same motivation, determination or sense of destiny that had inspired Babur, who never forgot that he had the 'blood of Timur' running through his veins. Rather, Humayan preferred to spend his time enjoying the life of the harem and creating a city of culture that would attract poets and philosophers from around the Muslim world. Despite his military failings he was cultured, amiable and extremely tolerant. Consequently, he was popular with the people and was often referred to as the 'Perfect Man'.

In 1537, Sultan Bahadur of Gujarat died in a battle against the Portuguese, but Sher Khan still remained a threat against which Humayan appeared impotent. Taking advantage of this weakness and also the fact that Humayan was on campaign in the East, his 19 years old brother Hindal seized control of Agra and proclaimed himself Emperor. At this point, his other brother Kamran, who ruled the Punjab, also marched on Agra to claim the throne. When Humayan discovered the treachery he surprisingly forgave his brothers and persuaded them to unite with him against Sher Khan. This is an example of his tolerant and forgiving personality that earned him the title 'Perfect Man'.

The brothers then wasted time arguing among themselves over battle tactics and all the while Sher Khan was gradually moving closer to the Mughal capital. Faced with the advancing armies, Humayan decided to retreat to Lahore. He would not return to his imperial capital for another 15 years.

Sher Shah Suri and the Sur Empire

Sher Khan's armies chased Humayan and his brothers as far as Lahore, forcing him to retreat even further eastwards. Humayan's brother Kamran denied him refuge in Kabul and so together with his immediate family and a small band of followers he travelled on into Sindh, Southern Pakistan, and finally into Persia. The year was 1540 and marked the end of Humayan's brief ten-year rule as Mughal Emperor in Delhi. This opened the way for Sher Khan to establish himself as Sher Shah Suri, Emperor of the Sur Empire in Northern India.

Sher Shah Suri was an ethnic Afghan of the Sur tribe. He was born Farid Khan in 1486 in Sasaram, Bihar. His father and grandfather had both held prominent positions in the government of the Lodi dynasty. When Babur defeated the Ibrahim Lodi in 1526, the region came under Mughal rule and the young Farid Khan found a position with the Mughal Governor of Bihar. In recognition of his bravery in battle the Governor renamed him Sher (lion) Khan. By 1534, Sher Khan had become ruler of Bihar. In 1539, at the Battle of Chausa, and again in 1540, at the Battle of Kannauj, he defeated the Mughal Emperor Humayan and his armies.

Sher Shah Suri's reign as Emperor of the Sur Empire marked something of a watershed in Indian history. While he was clearly a successful military leader, he was probably better known for his many administrative reforms.

One of his first acts, to mark his reign, was to introduce a new form of coinage. His silver coin was to be the first Indian rupee and he also minted gold and copper coins. He modernised the civil and military administrative system and established a postal service. He also renovated cities and completed monuments that had been started by Babur, for example, the Purana Qila, which is one of the oldest forts in Delhi and known today as the 'Old Fort'. At the time of the Partition of India, in August 1947, the fort was used as a refugee camp for hundreds of thousands of Muslims migrating to the newly founded State of Pakistan. Today the fort is used for theatrical performances and cultural events.

Apart from the rupee, another of Sher Shah Suri's legacies was the Grand Trunk Road that stretched across Northern India. During his reign he extended it from Chittagong in Bengal to Kabul in Afghanistan. In areas exposed to the sun he planted trees to provide travellers with shade and he also built caravanserais (highway inns) at regular intervals along the route. Because he wanted to encourage trade, much of the road was free of road tax.

Sher Shah Suri died in 1545 while fighting the Rajputs, which was a powerful Hindu dynasty. His magnificent mausoleum stands in the middle of an artificial lake in Sasaram, the town of his birth. Islam Shah Suri, his second son, succeeded as Emperor but the Empire only lasted until 1555, when the Mughals returned to Agra and succeeded in restoring their rule.

Humayan in Exile

Having been denied refuge in Kabul by his brother Kamal, Humayan's situation was worsened when many of the local Hindu rulers allied with Sher Shah Suri against him. He therefore decided to retreat further through the desert into Sindh where the Emir made him welcome. It was here, in an oasis garrison, that Humayan's young wife, Hamida Banu Begum, gave birth to a child. The date was the 15th October 1542 and the child was later to become Akbar the Great.

While in Sindh Humayan had the opportunity, with the help of the Emir, to strengthen his forces sufficiently to consider trying once more to regain his territory. But his way was barred by Kamal and he was forced to retreat to Kandahar. Here he made the decision to leave Afghanistan and seek refuge in Persia with the Safavid Shah Tahmasp. Because it was winter the journey was considered to be too dangerous for the young child and so he was left behind in Kandahar in the care of his paternal aunt.

It took Humayan, Hamida and a small group of followers a month to cross the mountains. It had been a gruelling journey but on arrival at Herat the small group of Mughals received a welcome worthy of their royal status.

While in Persia, Humayan had the opportunity to visit monuments that had been built by his Timurid ancestors and he enjoyed the sophisticated court life of the Safavids. Above all, he was introduced to the art and culture of Persia. He was particularly impressed with Persian miniature paintings and he met the most celebrated artists of the time.

Shah Tahmasp, who was supportive of the Mughals, offered to help Humayan take back his throne in Delhi. However, in return he asked that the Mughals should denounce their loyalty to Sunni Islam and convert to the Shi'a tradition of Islam that was the official religion of the Safavids. Initially Humayan was reluctant but, probably for pragmatic reasons, he finally agreed. The Shah also demanded that should Humayan succeed in regaining his empire, the city of Kandahar be handed over to the Persians.

Humayan decided to accept the help of the Safavids and return to Hindustan. Along with the necessary troops and munitions he was also accompanied by a large number of painters, poets and architects, all of whom would influence and contribute to the future culture of the Mughal Empire.

Humayan was able to retake both Kandahar and Kabul with relative ease, partly because many of Kamran's troops switched sides. They now preferred to ally themselves with Humayan, the legitimate Emperor, rather than his unpopular and oppressive brother. In November 1545, after an absence of three years, Humayan and Hamida were reunited with their son Akbar.

The Empire Restored

Following the death of Islam Shah Suri in 1554, several rivals for the throne of the Sur Empire marched on Delhi. This left the Sur dynasty in a weak position and Humayan decided that this would be the right time to take the Mughal throne back for himself. Realising that the task would be great and aware of his weak military skills, he put his armies under the able leadership of Bairam Khan who had been in the service of the Mughals since he was 16 years old.

On the 23rd July 1555, Humayan once more sat on the Mughal throne. With the death of his brothers he was now the undisputed ruler of the Empire. Furthermore, now having confidence in the loyalty of his generals, he was in a position to extend his territories in Eastern and Western India. He organised the migration of many Mughal families from Afghanistan to Hindustan and he planned further administrative reforms that would build on those introduced by Sher Shah Suri.

Unfortunately, Humayan did not live to see his plans fulfilled. On the 27th January 1556, he fell from the top floor of his library to his death. It is said that he was carrying a pile of books when he heard the call to prayer and in his rush to respond he caught his heel in his robes. He was 47 years old.

Soon after his death, Humayan's first wife and chief consort, Empress Bega Begum (also known as Haji Begum signifying her pilgrimage to Mecca) commissioned the building of a mausoleum for her husband. It was designed by a Persian architect of her own choice and was finally completed in 1572. Known as Humayan's Tomb, it was the first garden tomb on the Indian Subcontinent and the first monument to use red sandstone on such a large scale.

The tomb, which is part of a large complex including various monuments and gardens, also contains the graves of Bega Begum and numerous other Mughal rulers including Emperors Shah Jahan and Jahandar Shah. It is situated close to the *Purana*

Qila (Old Fort). During the Indian Uprising in 1857, the last Mughal Emperor Bahadur Shah sought refuge from the British in Humayan's tomb within confines of the tomb complex (see Chapter Eight).

Today Humayan's Tomb, along with the Taj Mahal, is visited by hundreds of thousands of people from around the world every year. It was declared a UNESCO World Heritage Site in 1993.

Conclusion

As the first son of Babur, Humayan inherited the throne on his father's death. However, in many ways he was not the best suited to rule an Empire. Despite his father's best efforts to prepare him for his future role, he was not by nature a shrewd strategist or an able military leader. Furthermore, his task was made particularly difficult since the Empire that he inherited had only been in existence for four years.

Humayan faced challenges early in his reign from members of the deposed Afghan Lodi dynasty, from the Emir of Gujarat and also the Afghan warlord Sher Khan. When his brothers Kamran and Hindal also turned against him he was forced to return to Afghanistan followed by exile in Persia. He had reigned for just ten years.

In many ways, the fifteen-year period of Humayan's exile was productive both for Hindustan under the Suri Empire and also for Humayan. During this time, Sher Shah Suri introduced reforms and embarked upon a building programme both of which Humayan would benefit from on his return to Delhi in 1555.

Humayan also gained from his period in Persia where he was introduced to Persian cultural and military life that not only enabled him to retake Delhi but also contribute to the cultural life of India. His agreement to accept Shi'a Islam as opposed to the Sunni tradition was most likely purely pragmatic in order to secure the help offered by Shah Tahmasp. Despite this, Shi'a Islam was to become a feature of the early Mughals and was to contribute to a religious tolerance less common within the Sunni tradition.

Humayan returned to Hindustan as a more able and more confident ruler. His period in Persia was also to be the foundation of what came to be a great synthesis of Persian, Islamic and Indian elements known as Indo-Islamic culture and architecture that was to be consolidated under his son Akbar the Great.

CHAPTER FOUR

Akbar the Great

Born in Exile

Abu'l Fath Jalal ud-din Muhammad Akbar, also known as Akbar, was born on the 15th October 1542 at Umerkot in present day Pakistan. After acceding to the Mughal throne in 1556, he gained the title Akbar the Great, which literally means Great the Great.

Akbar was born during the period when his father Humayan was seeking refuge in Afghanistan. Having been forced to leave Delhi by Sher Shah Suri, Humayan was denied protection in Kabul by his brother Kamran and he received a hostile reception from other Afghan tribal leaders in the region. When he decided to travel across the mountains into Persia with his young wife Hamida, the child Akbar was left in the care of his extended family in Kabul.

Under the tutelage of his uncles, Kamran and Askari, Akbar learned all the traditional skills that were expected of a royal descendent of Timur. Unlike his father, who had shown no interest in acquiring such skills, Akbar enjoyed the physical challenge of horsemanship and combat and at a young age he showed himself to be both daring and brave.

He did, however, share his father's interest in the pursuit of knowledge and particularly philosophy and religion. What is interesting is that whereas most of the royal household had been literate for generations, often composing poems and writing autobiographies, Akbar could neither read nor write. Consequently, throughout his life others would be required to read to him. Since his illiteracy could not be attributed to a lack of opportunity to learn, it is likely to have been the result of dyslexia or similar condition.

Akbar was only thirteen when his father died. As the eldest surviving son, he was the rightful heir to the throne, but his younger brothers still posed a threat. In the Turkic-Mongol tradition, succession often went to the son who seized the throne by force. The Turkic Ottomans faced the same problem. In the case of the Ottomans, the Sultan often gave his favourite son a governorship close to the imperial seat in Istanbul, while sending the other sons to far-flung outposts. This went some way towards ensuring that the favourite would be first to arrive and claim the throne.

Since Akbar was in a vulnerable position, Bairam Khan, the General appointed by Humayan to head the Mughal military, immediately took control. In many ways Bairam Khan had been the power behind the Mughal throne throughout Humayan's reign.

When Humayan died, Bairam Khan concealed the Emperor's death to give him sufficient time to prepare Akbar for enthronement. Just over two weeks after Humayan's death, on the 14th February 1556, Akbar succeeded as the third Mughal Emperor and Bairam Khan became Regent until Akbar came of age. While the Regency worked for a while, it was inevitable that eventually there would be friction between these two strong personalities. Akbar eventually offered Bairam Khan either retirement in the palace, or the opportunity to go on pilgrimage to Mecca, which was often a way of getting rid of difficult people. Bairam Khan chose the latter, but never did arrive in Mecca because he was assassinated in January 1561 while travelling through Gujarat.

The *Akbarnama*

The majority of the population of Hindustan had never placed much emphasis on the importance of history. As Hindus, a historical perspective had little place within their cyclical worldview of life, death and rebirth. Muslims, on the other hand, have always had a very strong sense of history. In common with Judaism and to a lesser extent Christianity, the Islamic worldview is founded upon historical events and particularly for Muslims, the life of the Prophet Muhammad who died in 632 AD. From that time, Muslim historians have recorded detailed accounts of major events in their history and Islamic scholars have, over the centuries, written vast theological treatises expounding the words and deeds of the Prophet.

Alongside history and theology, genealogy is also important for Muslims. The Shi'a, in particular, use genealogy in order to legitimise a succession that follows in a direct line of descent from the Prophet Muhammad. Genealogy also plays a part in Islamic theology where the authenticity of Koranic commentary, known as the Hadith, depends upon authentic sources that in turn must be supported by a lineage of received and reliable scholarship.

The importance of genealogy was evident in the life of Babur, the first Mughal Emperor. He was constantly reminded by his grandmother that he had the blood of Timur 'running through his veins', a mantra that enabled him to overcome numerous setbacks. Furthermore, it was probably Babur's sense of history that prompted him to write his own autobiography known as the *Baburnama,* meaning 'the story of Babur'.

Soon after Akbar came to the throne, he commissioned Abu al-Fazl to write his biography, that became known as the *Akbarnama.* As a court historian and biographer, Abu al-Fazl was one of Akbar's 'nine jewels'. These were the nine most prominent advisers of Akbar's Court.

Akbar also asked Gulbadan Begum, his aunt and the sister of Humayan, to write down as much as she could remember of her brother Humayan's life. His intention was that her memories, which became known as the *Humayan nama,* would include the period of Akbar's own early childhood and would contribute to the major work of Abu al-Fazl.

The *Akbarnama* was written in Persian and it is said that it took some seven years to complete with over forty artists working on the many paintings that illustrated the text. It is divided into three volumes. The first volume details the history of the Timurids, the reigns of Babur and Humayan and the birth of Akbar. The second volume describes the reign of Akbar and the third volume gives fascinating and detailed information about the administration and organisation of the Empire as well as a description of Hinduism.

The manuscript remained with the Mughals until it came into the possession of the British Commissioner of Oudh in around 1860. It was then bought by the South Kensington Museum in 1896 and is currently held in the Victoria and Albert Museum.

The *Baburnama, Humayan nama* and *Akbarnama* provide a unique insight into the life and times of the first three Mughal Emperors. All three manuscripts have subsequently been translated into English and are now available in digital form.

Military Achievements

Babur's foothold in Hindustan had only lasted four years and Humayan had struggled throughout his reign to hold onto both Delhi and Agra. When Akbar acceded to the throne in 1556, his priorities were first to secure Mughal territory already held and second, to consolidate and expand his Empire.

His first challenge came from Hemu, a Hindu general leading the forces of a local Afghan warlord who wanted to unseat the young Akbar. On the 5th November 1556, at what is known as the Second Battle of Panipat, the Mughal army under the leadership of Bairam Khan defeated Hemu. This was an important battle in that it marked the end of any further outside threat and the beginning of a successful period of Mughal expansion.

After having secured Delhi and Agra, and with the help of Bairam Khan, Akbar then secured the loyalty of all the remaining Afghan tribes of the Punjab. He now believed it was time to bring the entire royal family and those of his nobles and generals, from Kabul and Kandahar to Hindustan. This sent a clear message that he intended to stay in Delhi.

There was a break in the campaigning in 1559 due to disagreements with Bairam Khan. Akbar's relatives and especially his foster mother Maham Angar, put pressure on him to get rid of the man who had stood by his side throughout most of his life. When Bairam Khan chose to go on pilgrimage to Mecca, rather than spend his retirement at court, it was with a heavy heart that Akbar let him go, especially so when he heard of his assassination soon after. Akbar then went on to marry Bairam Khan's widow.

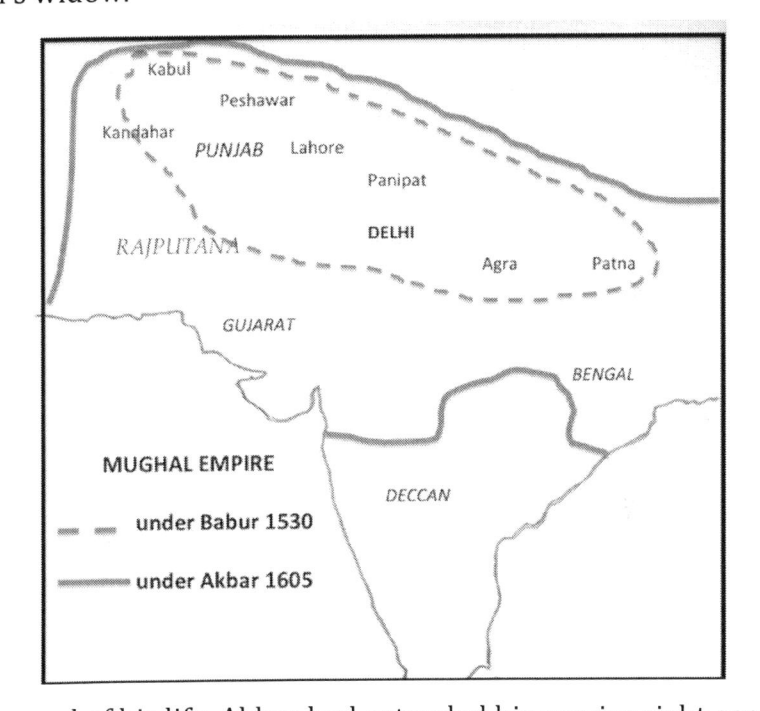

```
Kabul
Peshawar
Kandahar
PUNJAB  Lahore
        Panipat
        DELHI
RAJPUTANA
        Agra    Patna
GUJARAT
                BENGAL
MUGHAL EMPIRE
                DECCAN
— — under Babur 1530
——— under Akbar 1605
```

By the end of his life, Akbar had extended his empire right across Northern India and down towards the Deccan. Some of his fiercest resistance came early in his reign, from the proud and warlike Rajputs of Hindu Rajputana. In the Rajput State of Gondwara resistance came from Rani (Queen) Durgavati who personally led her troops against the might of the Mughals. She was injured in the battle and rather than retreat or face capture, she chose to commit suicide by stabbing herself with her dagger. Rani Durgavati is still celebrated in India for her bravery and in 1983 the University of Jabalpur was renamed 'Rani Durgavati Vishwavidyalaya' in her honour.

Akbar faced another formidable woman in 1595 when he attacked the Deccan state of Ahmadnagar. In this case Chand Bibi, the Regent Queen, also personally led her army but she was forced to admit defeat.

Akbar preferred diplomacy rather than force when dealing with the Rajputs. In the time-honoured tradition of the Timurids, he strengthened his relationship with them by marrying a Rajput princess, Mariam-uz-Zamini. Marrying into the family of opponents was also common practice in Europe at the time, particularly during the medieval period of the Holy Roman Empire. However, Akbar went much further. First, he invited all the Hindu relatives of his new wife to move into his palace and second, he gave the ablest of the Rajput Generals senior positions in his army.

Reform

Akbar's military successes were partly due to his superior munitions. With the help of both the Ottomans and the Portuguese, he was able to acquire the most up to date matchlock rifles and the latest cannons, which gave him an advantage over his enemies.

He also reorganised the Mansabdari system that had been practiced by the Mongols and used by both Babur and Humayan. The word Mansab has its origins in Arabic and means rank or position and it related to both military and civil life.

Within the military, each Mansab was responsible for the training and discipline of a certain number of soldiers. There were 33 ranks with the most senior officer being responsible for 10,000 men while the most junior had just ten men under his command. Only the Princes and most important Rajput leaders were given a Mansab of 10,000 men. The army was then split into various divisions: cavalry, infantry, elephants, artillery and navy.

As with the feudal system in medieval Europe, each Mansab was expected to pay for the upkeep of his own horses. In the case of the Mughals, this also included elephants. A stipulated number of horses, elephants, camels, mules, carts, etc. was allocated according to rank. All horses were branded to avoid corruption and for every ten cavalrymen twenty horses had to be maintained, so allowing the animals time to rest while on the march or to ensure replacements in time of war.

Throughout his life, Akbar took a keen interest in the military and the question of discipline. For example, the Emperor made all appointments, awarded promotions or declared demotions. He also fixed all salaries, which were generous. He kept a close eye on discipline and the death penalty could only be carried out with his written permission.

The Mansabdari system also applied to civil life. Instead of receiving a salary, nobles were granted a portion of land, determined by rank, called a Jagir. The land then provided revenue from which a salary was taken, the remainder of the income going to the royal treasury. In some cases, the nobles were also expected to perform military duty. A Jagir was not hereditary and at the time of death the land reverted to the State. The system continued throughout the period of the Mughals and was still in use under the British East India Company. In 1951, four years after achieving Independence, the Indian Government abolished the system.

Religious Policy

Akbar has gone down in history as being the most religiously tolerant of all the Mughal Emperors. Soon after his accession, he introduced reforms to address religious discrimination. He permitted Hindu custom and law to be used by the judiciary when a Hindu was facing prosecution. He abolished the Pilgrimage Tax for Hindus as well as the Jizya tax that is normally placed on all non-Muslims living under Islamic rule.

He also decreed that Hindus who had converted to Islam under duress should be permitted to return to their religion without fear of persecution, which in Islam was usually the death penalty under the law of apostasy. He also discouraged child marriage and encouraged the remarriage of widows. This latter policy may well have been an attempt to redress the Hindu practice of suttee whereby a widow was expected to voluntarily place herself on her dead husband's funeral pyre.

Within his own family circle, as mentioned earlier, he welcomed the relatives of his Hindu wife into the palace and made no attempt to convert anyone to Islam. He encouraged the building of Hindu, Jain and Sikh temples as well as Churches for Christians. It was Akbar who granted land to the Sikhs at Amritsar in order that they could build what became the Golden Temple.

Although the Mughals were nominally Sunnis, Emperors Babur, Humayan and especially Akbar were strongly influenced by Sufism and Shi'ism. This was probably a consequence of their close relationship with the Persian Safavids for whom Shi'a Islam was the State religion. Humayan's 'conversion' to Shi'ism mentioned in the previous chapter will also have had an effect on the royal household.

Shi'ism is generally less conservative than the Sunni tradition and this is reflected in the early Mughals' acceptance of religious diversity. Akbar displayed not only a religious tolerance but he was also interested in spiritual matters and was a devotee of Shaikh Salim Chishti, the great Sufi teacher.

He was also genuinely interested in the beliefs of non-Muslims. In 1575, he built the 'Ibadat Khana' (House of Worship) at Fatehpur Sikri, the city he founded in Agra in 1569, in order that he could invite theologians from different religions to take part in inter religious dialogue. Apart from Sufis, Sikhs, Jains and Hindus he invited Jesuit priests. His hope was that through debate the theologians would overcome their differences, share what they had in common and live together in equality.

Underpinning Akbar's policies on religion was a sincere desire to overcome sectarianism, which he believed would ultimately help to unify and therefore strengthen his Empire. In the 4th Century, the Roman Emperor Constantine saw the advantages of uniting his vast Empire under the official religion of Christianity and Akbar attempted to do something similar.

When his efforts to bring theologians together in dialogue frequently ended up in argument and even abuse, he opted for a more radical solution. He decided to found his own religion, known as Din-i Ilahi (Religion of God). Believing that no religion held the monopoly of truth, he brought together what he thought to be the best elements of all. Not surprisingly he upset the

Mullahs of the religious establishment who accused him of blasphemy. However, the Din-i Ilahi only attracted a few supporters from within the palace and did not survive beyond Akbar's death.

The Jesuits

In May 1498, Vasco da Gama discovered a sea route between Portugal and the Malabar Coast of the Indian sub-continent. Six years later the Portuguese Overseas Empire, known as Portuguese India, was founded at Cochin and in 1510 its capital was transferred to Goa. This independent Portuguese State was to last for over four hundred years, until 1961, when it was finally annexed by India.

In 1542, Francis Xavier, one of the original founders of the Society of Jesus, also known as the Jesuits, arrived in Goa. He spent three years in India mainly instructing the growing number of Portuguese settlers in the Faith, many who were said to be fraternising with the local heathen Hindu population. During this time, he sought the conversion of Hindus and was instrumental in establishing the Portuguese Inquisition, which was an extension of the Spanish Inquisition, the aim of which was to seek out heresy.

Following Xavier's departure to China, other Jesuit priests arrived in Goa to continue his work. By the time of Akbar's reign, the Portuguese presence along the western coast of India was significant and Akbar was well aware of the work of the Jesuits.

We have an excellent account of the relationship between Akbar and the Jesuits from Father Pierre du Jarric S J's contemporary work, *Akbar and the Jesuits.* The manuscript was translated with an Introduction by C H Payne and first published in 1926. The book gives detailed information about Akbar's court, his personality and particularly his hospitality and thirst for knowledge.

According to the author, the first Portuguese Ambassadors from Goa arrived at Akbar's court in 1578. Their manners and behaviour impressed the Emperor and he was extremely curious about their Faith. As well as the arrival the Portuguese, Ambassadors from the Court of Queen Elizabeth I also visited Akbar, hoping to secure trade concessions for the English similar to those granted to the Portuguese.

Soon after the visit of the Portuguese Ambassadors, Akbar sent a letter to the Head of the Order of the Jesuits in Goa requesting that:

"...you send me two Fathers, learned in the scriptures, who shall bring with them the principal books of the law, and of the Gospels; for I have a great desire to become acquainted with this law and its perfection....Know, also, that the Fathers who shall come here will be received by me with all honour, and that it will be a peculiar pleasure to me to see them. If, after I have been instructed as I desire in their law and its perfection, they wish to return, they will be free to do so whenever it shall seem good to them, and I shall despatch them with great respect and honour. Let them not hesitate to come, for they will be under my care and protection."

In response, three priests were sent to Akbar's court in the hope that their endeavours may result in the conversion of the Emperor to Christianity.

This was to be the beginning of a Jesuit presence at the court that lasted throughout Akbar's life. During this time, he spent many hours with the priests, learning the Portuguese language and being instructed in the Christian Faith. He also arranged debates between the Jesuits and his Mullahs and according to Jarric, the priests, who were highly educated and skilful with words, outwitted the Mullahs on every occasion.

Initially, due to the enthusiasm with which Akbar responded to what he heard, the Jesuits were hopeful that their mission might be accomplished. But while Akbar acknowledged the many positive things about Christianity, he was troubled by both the Doctrine of the Trinity and the Incarnation, both of which were totally alien to his strict monotheistic views. The sticking point was always the idea of God having a son. Akbar was also disappointed that the priests were unable to perform miracles in the name of Jesus.

Despite his misgivings, he continued to study the Scriptures and show the priests the greatest of respect. He ensured that they were well accommodated and he arranged for a Church and school to be built for their use. He also permitted them to evangelise among the Muslims and to conduct baptisms.

Not surprisingly, Akbar's close relationship with the Jesuits attracted criticism, not only from the Mullahs, but also from the female members of his household. They were fearful that should he convert to Christianity all but one would be banished from the palace.

Eventually it became clear that Akbar had no intention of changing his Faith. Although the mission of the Jesuits might have come to an end at that point, he insisted that they should remain at his court in order to instruct his sons. Although the original Fathers returned to Goa, others took their place. All hopes were now placed on the conversion of Akbar's sons and heirs.

Akbar died on the 27th October 1605 after an unexpected, and prolonged bout of dysentery. He was succeeded by his eldest surviving son, Mirza Nur-ud-din Beig Mohammad Khan Selim, known as Selim before his enthronement and thereafter as Jahangir, Conqueror of the World.

In his memoires, Jahangir described his father as follows:

In stature he was of medium height. He had a wheaten complexion and black eyes and eyebrows. His countenance was radiant, and he had the build of a lion, broad of chest with long hands and arms....His august voice was very loud, and he had a particularly nice way of speaking."

Conclusion

Although the story of the Mughals can be traced back to Genghis Khan and Timur, the reign of Akbar the Great marks the beginning of Mughal power in the full sense of Empire. Under Akbar, Mughal territory was extended from Kandahar in the West, to Bengal in the East. Akbar also conquered the region of

Gujarat, which gave him not only access to the vital seaports, but also control of the seas of the Indian Ocean.

He wisely chose diplomacy over force when it came to the warlike Rajputs, with whom he formed an alliance that was strengthened by marriage contracts. In this way, he was able to bring experienced Rajput warriors into his own army.

Apart from his many military achievements, Akbar is rightly remembered for his enlightened reforms, many of which were aimed at redressing religious discrimination across the Empire.

Being a sincere devotee of the Sufi Saint Chishti, Akbar showed a genuine disposition towards spirituality. He also displayed a thirst for knowledge of other religious traditions and encouraged theologians of all traditions to engage in inter religious debate.

However, it is difficult to know the degree to which this was simply inter religious engagement for its own sake or as a means of uniting and strengthening his Empire. Akbar was a pragmatist and he knew that stability was dependent upon good relations between all religious and ethnic communities. It is likely therefore that his reforms and policies were worked out with this in mind.

Equally, Akbar probably had ulterior motives when he invited the Jesuits to instruct him in the Christian Faith. He was a Timurid, a conqueror at heart and had ambitions to extend his empire southwards towards Goa and beyond. He was shrewd and knew that conquest was not simply a matter of force. As he had proven with the Rajputs, diplomacy was preferable. His invitation to the Jesuits was as much about gaining valuable intelligence about this alien Christian State as it was about learning about Christianity.

Due to his enlightened views, Akbar's reign marks the high point of religious tolerance in Mughal history. Together with his administrative and military achievements, he well deserves the title, 'Akbar and Great'.

CHAPTER FIVE

Jahangir, Conqueror of the World

The *Jahangirnama*

Following in the tradition of the first three Mughal Emperors, Jahangir's life was recorded in the *Jahangirnama* (the story of Jahangir). In common with his great grandfather Babur, he wrote it himself, whereas the *Humayan nama* and *Akbarnama* were commissioned works. However, since Jahangir only wrote about the first fifteen years of his reign, the work was taken up by Muhammad-Hadi who, in his own words, had been *'enamored of the science of history and the craft of biography from the time the breeze of youth began to blow'*.

In the process of gathering the various manuscripts together, Muhammad-Hadi came to realise that there were significant gaps in the early part of the autobiography. He therefore wrote his own account of the period from Jahangir's birth, in August 1569, to his accession to the throne in October 1605. The *Jahangirnama* was written in Persian, the language of the Mughal Court and in some editions Muhammad-Hadi's work appears as a Preface, while in others as an Appendix.

Apart from the official biographies of the court historians, we have letters and reports written by European traders and diplomats. The diaries of Sir Thomas Roe, Ambassador to the Mughal Court from 1615 to 1618, are particularly enlightening. Apparently, he had a very good relationship with Jahangir, which gave him a unique insight into court life.

From Birth to Accession

Muhammad-Hadi begins his Preface with an account of Jahangira's illustrious lineage that went back as far as Timur. He then goes on to describe how his father, the 27-year old Akbar, had been desperate for a son and heir, especially since his firstborn twin sons, Hassan and Husain, had died in infancy. In his despair, Akbar had frequently consulted astronomers and he sought help from the Sufi Shaykh Salim.

Believing that the pregnancy of Akbar's Hindu wife Mariam-uz-Zamani was an answer to prayer, she was sent to the Shaykh's house in the town of Sikri, in the vicinity of Agra, for her confinement. In thanksgiving for the safe delivery of a son, who was to be the future Jahangir, Akbar commissioned the building of a great city at Sikri. It became known as Fatehpur Sikri and was the Mughal capital from 1571 to 1585. Today it is one of the many Mughal sites visited by people from around the world. As a further mark of thanksgiving, Akbar also distributed money to the people and gave orders that all prisoners in the Empire should be released.

Jahangir was born Mirza Nur-ud-din Beig Mohammad Khan Salim, the name Salim being in honour of Shaykh Salim. Until his accession as Emperor he was known as Salim, or Selim. But he was uncomfortable with this name because it could be confused with the Ottoman Sultan Selim, known as the Grim, on account of his aggressive expansionist policies. On his accession, Salim chose the name Jahangir, which in Persian means 'Conqueror of the World'.

In accordance with ancient custom, Prince Salim started his education when he was four years, four months and four days old and being the heir to the throne he studied under the finest tutors. He excelled in languages and from an early age showed a great interest in the arts. When he was just eight years old he was awarded the rank of 10,000 mansab, as befitting his princely status.

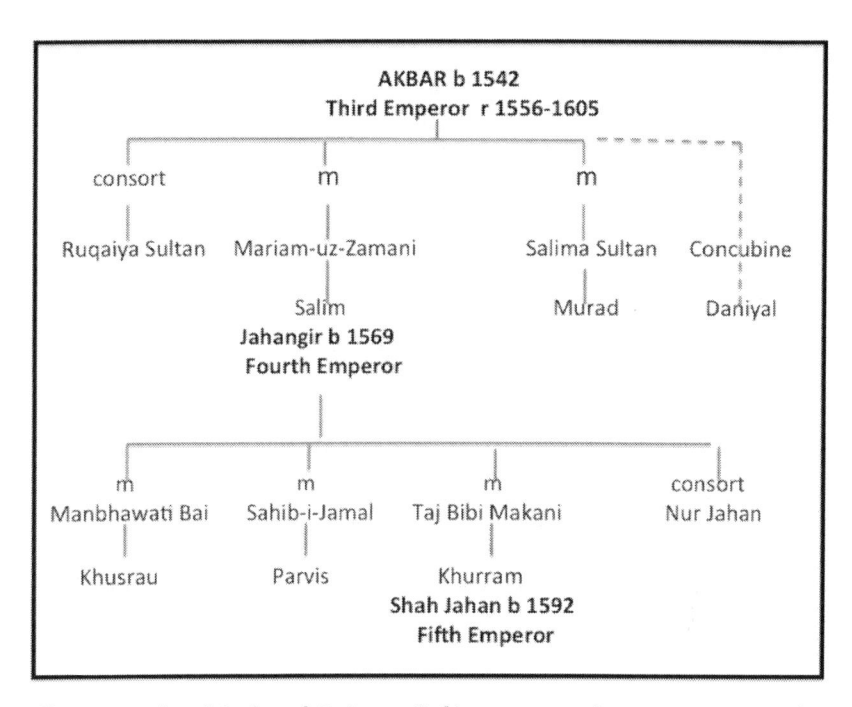

```
                    AKBAR b 1542
              Third Emperor  r 1556-1605
    ┌──────────────┬──────────────┬──────────────┐
  consort          m              m           (concubine)
    │              │              │              │
Ruqaiya Sultan  Mariam-uz-Zamani  Salima Sultan  Concubine
                   │              │              │
                 Salim          Murad          Daniyal
               Jahangir b 1569
               Fourth Emperor
    ┌──────────────┬──────────────┬──────────────┐
    m              m              m           consort
Manbhawati Bai  Sahib-i-Jamal  Taj Bibi Makani  Nur Jahan
    │              │              │
 Khusrau        Parvis         Khurram
                              Shah Jahan b 1592
                              Fifth Emperor
```

Following the birth of Prince Salim, two other sons were born: Prince Murad in 1570 and Prince Daniyal in 1572. Both Princes received part of their education from the Jesuit priests (See previous chapter). Apart from Christianity, Prince Murad also studied Buddhism and was said to be the first person to follow the *Din-e-Ilahi*, the syncretic religion founded by Akbar.

Murad, who was born to Salima Sultan Begum, one of Akbar's chief wives, was described as *"..dark, and he was tall in stature, inclining to be portly. Gravity was apparent in his manner, and bravery and manliness were evident from his conduct."*

Daniyal was the son of a one of Akbar's concubines. In his memoires, Jahangir describes him as *"a young man of fine stature, with a pleasing build and good-looking. He was very fond of elephants and horses...He was fond of Indian singing. Occasionally he composed poetry in the language and idiom of the people of India that wasn't bad"*

Akbar was to be disappointed in his sons, largely because they put their personal pleasures before the needs of the Empire.

Babur and Humayan had to fight to hold onto their territory and Akbar had to use all his military skills in order to consolidate and expand the Empire. Akbar's sons, on the other hand, were born at a time of prolonged stability with no serious threat from outside invasion. Consequently, the princes were able to enjoy the wealth, luxury and leisure time denied to the earlier Mughal rulers. Rather than learning the art of war, they excelled in the art of debauchery, including an excess of wine, women and opium. Both Murad and Daniyal died from alcohol poisoning, Murad at 28 years and Daniyal at 31 years.

Prince Salim, the future Emperor Jahangir, also consumed too much wine and was addicted to opium. He also enjoyed poetry, literature and painting and was probably the greatest of the Mughal Emperors as a patron of the arts.

He was known to spend too much time in the company of women and his name has been linked in an illicit affair to Anarkali, whose identity is unclear. Some believe that she was a slave, or dancing girl and was possibly the mother of Daniyal. If she were the mother of Daniyal, then she would have been both his father's concubine and his aunt. Not surprisingly, there is no mention of this shameful affair in either the *Akbarnama* or *Jahangirnama*, works that were primarily written with the aim of glorifying the lives of the Emperors.

An English trader named William Finch, of the East India Company, was the first to make reference to the affair. In 1608, Finch and Captain Hawkins landed at Surat on the coast of Gujarat. They spent about eighteen months at the Mughal Court at a time when arrangements were being made for the first English Ambassador, Sir Thomas Roe, to take up his post at the Court. After much negotiation, Emperor Jahangir finally issued a *Firman* authorising the East India Company to set up a factory at Surat, in competition with the Portuguese.

Sir Thomas Roe, who was on relatively good terms with Jahangir, was also hoping to gain further trade concessions, or 'capitulations' similar to those obtained from the Ottomans. According to Roe's reports, his draft Treaty:

'provided for the free access of the English to all ports belonging to the Great Mogul, including those of Bengal and Sind, and the free passage of their goods without payment of any duty beyond the usual customs; they were to be allowed to buy and sell freely, to rent factories, to hire boats and carts, and to buy provisions at the usual rates...'

This was to be the first foothold of a British presence that would eventually rule India.

Whether or not there is any truth in the story of Prince Salim's love affair with Anarkali, it is a romantic tale and has caught the imagination of Indians ever since. It has been the subject of numerous Indian films, plays and TV series.

Following the deaths of Princes Murad and Daniyal, Akbar placed all hope on Salim and he was reluctant to believe the stories that were being circulated about his son's lifestyle. Even when Mariam-uz-Zamani, his wife and the mother of Salim, warned him about the Prince's behaviour, he ignored her warnings, hoping they were based on rumour.

Akbar's trusted advisers, and particularly Abdul Fazl, were also critical of Salim's behaviour and they had doubts as to his suitability to take over the role of Emperor. Prince Salim and Abdul Fazl had a poor relationship and Salim believed, with some justification, that Abdul Fazl would do all he could to discredit him in the eyes of his father. His solution was to arrange the assassination of Abdul Fazl. He assigned the task to Raja Bir Singh Deo, who willingly murdered Abdul Fazl and then sent his head to Salim. Although Akbar was distraught at the death of his long-trusted friend and adviser, it appears that he did not, or would not, believe that Salim had any part in it.

Salim also had a reputation for cruelty. On one particular occasion, when he ordered the flaying alive of a miscreant, the Emperor is reported as saying *"We have conquered a whole world by the sword, but until today we have not ordered so much as a sheep to be skinned in our presence! My son is unimaginably hard-hearted if he can have a man skinned in his presence."*

The relationship between Akbar and his son gradually deteriorated, largely because Salim was impatient for power. By the age of 30 years, he believed he was ready to rule the Empire but Akbar, by then around 60 years, appeared to be as fit and able as ever. When Akbar died in 1605 from a sudden bout of dysentery, it led some to speculate that the cause of death was poisoning and that possibly Salim was implicated in his father's death.

Salim becomes Emperor Nur-ud-din Muhammad Jahangir

On the 15th October 1605, Prince Salim ascended the throne. He chose his own name for Emperor and he placed the imperial crown on his own head. The concept of monarchy is incompatible with the precepts of Islam and when the Mughal Emperors ascended the throne, while there was great celebration, there was little in the way of ceremony or ritual compared to the coronation of European monarchs. For the Mughals, and also the Ottomans, the most powerful symbol of power was the 'girding of the sword'. The Mughals also placed great importance on the 'donation of the robe'.

Jahangir describes in detail his first acts as Emperor. He tells us that he first commissioned the manufacture of a chain made out of solid gold and containing sixty bells. One end was fixed to the tower of his palace and the other to the banks of the nearby river. It was called the Chain of Justice and the idea was that any citizen with a grievance would be able to 'summons' the Emperor simply by pulling at the chain.

He also promulgated twelve new decrees, all of which were aimed at improving the lives of the people. For example, he ordered that landowners should build caravanserai and mosques along desolate roads for the benefit of travellers. He declared that all property of a deceased person, even a non-Muslim, should be passed on to their heirs.

He declared that: *"no wine, spirits or any sort of intoxicant or forbidden liquor is to be manufactured or sold."* He then tells us in his memoires, *"This despite the fact that I myself commit the sin of drinking wine."* He also decreed that the slaughter of animals was to be forbidden on Thursday and Sunday of every week.

It is debateable as to how effective these laws were. Nevertheless, they were a gesture of goodwill towards the people. As is always the case, it is one thing to pass a law, but quite another to be able to enforce it.

Jahangir then goes to great lengths to describe how he awarded Governorships and gave out promotions to loyal servants of the Empire. Women of the royal harem also received a greater personal allowance.

Prince Khusrau

Jahangir's first son, Khusrau, was born to his first wife, Manbhawati Bai, in August 1587. At the time of Jahangir's ascension, Khusrau was 18 years old and according to his father, *"corrupting notions had crept into Khusraw's head because of his youth and the conceit that afflicts the young".* Jahangir also says in his memoirs that Khusrau's behaviour had led his mother to commit suicide by an overdose of opium.

However, this was not the view of Khrusrau's grandfather Akbar. The boy had been his favourite grandson and as his own relationship with Salim continued to deteriorate, the Emperor started to put his hopes for the future of the dynasty in his grandson.

Others in the court also favoured Khusrau. Shortly after Jahangir's accession, a plot was hatched to overthrow him and put the young Khusrau, who would simply be a puppet Emperor, on the throne.

On the 6th April 1606, just sixth months after Jahangir's accession, Khusrau left Agra with around 3,000 horsemen. He claimed to be going to visit Akbar's tomb but in reality, he was heading for Lahore. As he passed through Panipat, other rebels joined him and while passing through Amitsar, he was received by the Sikh Guru Arjun Dev.

Jahangir soon discovered the rebellion and immediately set off with the imperial army. Khusrau was eventually captured while trying to cross the river Chenab. The rebellious son was taken to Delhi along with his supporters. He was placed on an elephant and forced to watch the impalement of his comrades. On the orders of his father, he was then blinded and imprisoned at Agra. His younger brother, Prince Khurram, the future Emperor Shah Jahan, ordered his execution in 1622.

Guru Arjan

Jahangir was also determined to punish Guru Arjan, who was the fifth of the ten Sikh Gurus. He believed that the Guru had supported Khusrau in his rebellion and so had him taken to Lahore fort where he died. The exact cause of his death is unclear. Some believe that he was tortured to death for refusing to convert to Islam. Another theory is that he was drowned.

Whatever the truth may be, Sikhs view his death as martyrdom and the event was a turning point in Sikh history. From that moment, Sikhs were ordered to take up armed resistance against Islamic persecution, symbolised ever since by the wearing of the *kirpan*, or sword. This event also marks the beginning of an uncomfortable relationship between Islam and Sikhism that has continued to this day.

Nur Jahan, the Light of the World

Jahangir's first wife was Manbhawati Bai, mother of Khusrau, who he married at the age of fifteen. Estimates vary as to how many other wives he had. Current thinking is that he probably had twenty wives and as many as 300 concubines. In 1611, at the age of 42, he married Nur Jahan. She was to become not only his greatest love, but also the true power behind the throne.

Nur Jahan was born in Kandahar in 1577. Named Mihrunnisa, she was the daughter of a Persian noble who migrated to India where he quickly rose up through the ranks of the Mughal court to finally become Grand Vizier.

Jahangir gave his new 34 years old bride a favoured position from the outset. He first named her Nur Mahal, meaning 'Light of the Palace' but as her status grew, he renamed her Nur Jahan, meaning 'Light of the World'.

Nur Jahan was famed for not only her beauty but for her many other talents. She was a gifted artist, fabric designer and interior decorator. She was also interested in architecture and commissioned a white marble mausoleum for her father that was to be a forerunner of the Taj Mahal. Jahangir and Nur Jahan often went hunting together and she had a reputation for her bravery and marksmanship. It is said that on one occasion she shot four tigers with just six bullets.

The Empress is described as having large eyes, a broad forehead and a high- bridged nose. It is said that she had a firm chin and small, but well-shaped mouth. Jahangir commissioned many portraits of Nur Jahan and given his artistic eye, it is likely that they were a fair portrayal.

As Nur Jahan's power increased, Jahangir slowly retreated into the background. This was partly due to a gradual decline in health, probably the result of a life of excess. Consequently, he passed more and more of the affairs of state over to his wife. Coin was struck in her name and 'Nur Jahan, the Queen Begum' was added to that of Jahangir on all *Firmans* and state documents.

Not surprisingly, this caused resentment among some at the court, which was aggravated by the fact that members of Nur Jahan's family were given key positions in the administration of the Empire.

Rebellion of Prince Khurram

As mentioned earlier, Jahangir's first son Khusrau, was blinded and imprisoned as punishment for trying to seize the throne from his father in 1605. His second son, Parviz, was weak and indecisive and not considered to be a serious contender for succession. This left the third son, Khurram, as favourite.

Jahangir and Nur Jahan did not have a child of their own, but she had two children from a previous marriage; a daughter, Ladli Begum and a son Shazada Kamal. In order to secure her influence into future generations and beyond the life of Jahangir, she arranged for Ladli to marry Shahryar, a younger son of Jahangir and she arranged for her niece, the future Mumtaz Mahal, to marry Prince Khurram.

By around 1620, Jahangir's health was in serious decline and Nur Jahan was in complete control of the Empire in all but name. When the Persians attacked Kandahar, she ordered Prince Khurram to go and defend the city, probably with the intention of sending him as far away from the court as possible. However, Khurram probably saw through the plot and was therefore reluctant to be away from Agra at a time when his father's health was failing. He suspected, probably rightly, that in his absence Nur Jahan would poison the mind of Jahangir against him in favour of her son-in-law, Shahryar. Furthermore, it was never wise for the heir to the throne to be away from the imperial seat when the Emperor's life was in danger.

Despite Nur Jahan's orders, Prince Khurram decided not to go to Kandahar and consequently the city was lost to the Persians. Instead, he raised an army to march against the Imperial forces. For the next three years, father and son were in armed conflict but eventually Khurram was forced into unconditional surrender.

Unlike his treatment of his first rebellious son, some twenty years earlier, who was blinded and imprisoned, Jahangir was surprisingly lenient with Khurram. He was awarded the governorship of Balaghat in Central India where he bided his time until he ascended the throne at the death of Jahangir in 1628.

Following Jahangir's death and having failed to get her son-in-law on the throne, Nur Jahan spent the rest of her life with her daughter Lladi. She occupied her time writing Persian poetry and overseeing the construction of her father's mausoleum, known as Itmad-Ud-Daulah's Tomb. She died at the age of 68 and is buried at Lahore.

Conclusion

Jahangir, the fourth Mughal Emperor, inherited an Empire that was relatively stable and free from outside threat. Unlike the earlier Mughal Emperors, he was not forced into serious military action to defend his territory, nor did he show any ambition towards territorial expansion. If ever his forces were mobilised, it was normally to put down an internal rebellion.

With stability came a period of increasing wealth and Jahangir, with his great love of arts and fondness for jewellery, epitomised the Mughal court at its most resplendent. Indeed, he has often been described as the 'Treasury of the World', reflecting the vast number of gems with which he was adorned.

As a young man Jahangir, and his younger brothers, over-indulged in wine, women and opium. However, whereas Murad and Daniyal had both died from alcohol poisoning, Jahangir was able to curb these excesses. He tells us in his memoirs that he did not drink until the age of eighteen. But then, while on campaign, he was offered some 'alcohol syrup' to cure his exhaustion. He says:

"I drank it and liked the feeling I got. After that I started drinking wine, increasing it day by day until I no longer got a kick out of grape wine and started drinking liquor." When warned that he was in danger of killing himself, he says: *"From that date I began to decrease the amount and.... ordered the spirits to be mixed with grape wine'.*

On his accession, Jahangir continued with his father's policies and also introduced new reforms. However, he fell short when it came to maintaining good interreligious relations, which had been so important to Akbar. For example, he dealt brutally with Guru Arjun, the Fifth Sikh Guru. To this day, Sikhs consider the death of Guru Arjun, at the hands of Jahangir, to be an act of martyrdom, that resulted in a deterioration in relations between Muslims and Sikhs.

Compared with his father, Jahangir had a cruel streak in him, exemplified by the punishments he meted out to those who supported his rebellious son Khusrau. However, as the years went by, he seems to have mellowed somewhat. His treatment, later in his reign, towards his other rebellious son, Khurram, was quite different.

It could well be that Jahangir's 'mellowing' was a reflection of his general withdrawal from life, as his powerful wife Nur Jahan increasingly took control. On the other hand, if his intention was that Khurram should succeed him as Emperor, it would be counter-productive to cause him too much harm.

Jahangir chose the title 'Conqueror of the World' when he ascended the throne at the age of 46 years. But although he hardly deserved the title 'conqueror', he did appear to have the wellbeing of the Empire and its peoples at heart.

Whatever failings he may have had, Jahangir has gone down in history as one of the most popular of the Mughal Emperors. This is probably because of his honesty and human frailties that come across in his memoirs as well as his vulnerability in the hands of a powerful woman. He was a man to whom many could relate.

CHAPTER SIX
Shah Jahan, King of the World

The Biographies

Shah Jahan, the fifth Mughal Emperor, chose not to write his own biography, but to commission his various court historians to undertake the work. The first historian to be given the task was Muhammad Amin Kazwini, sometimes known as Mirza Amina. His biography, known as the *Padshah-Nama*, covers the period from Shah Jahan's (Khurram's) birth to accession and the first ten year's rule as Emperor. Kazwini says that he intended to write an account of the second ten years, but for some reason this did not materialise. However, Kazwini's biography was to provide a model for later biographies.

Abdul Hamid Lahori wrote a second biography, known as the *Badshah-nama*. Lahori claims that the Emperor chose him because he was able to write in the style of the famed Abdul Fazl, author of the *Akbar-nama.*

Inyat Khan, who was born in the year that Shah Jahan came to the throne, wrote a third biography. For a period, he was employed as superintendent of the Imperial Library and while there he gained access to the works of Kazwini and Lahori, both of which he found difficult. In the preface to his own biography he says:

'The author desires to observe that the style of these volumes [Kazwini and Lahori] *seemed difficult and diffuse to his simple mind...'* and *'it would be well for him to write the history of the reign of Shah Jahan in a simple and clear style ... in plain language and in a condensed form.'*

All the biographies cover similar events: the most important military campaigns of Shah Jahan's reign and detailed information about appointments and promotions. In common with biographies of the earlier Emperors, the aim was always to portray a powerful ruler who was also just and generous in his dealings with his people. Because Shah Jahan had several biographers, each covering similar ground, there were also subtle differences.

We get a different perspective of the Mughals from the writings of the various diplomats and employees of the East India Company. Sir Thomas Roe, English Ambassador to the Mughal Court, when speaking of the young Shah Jahan, said *'I never saw so settled a countenance, nor any man keepe so constant a gravity, never smiling, or in face showing any respect or difference of men, but mingled with extreme pride and contempt of all.'*

The Young Princes

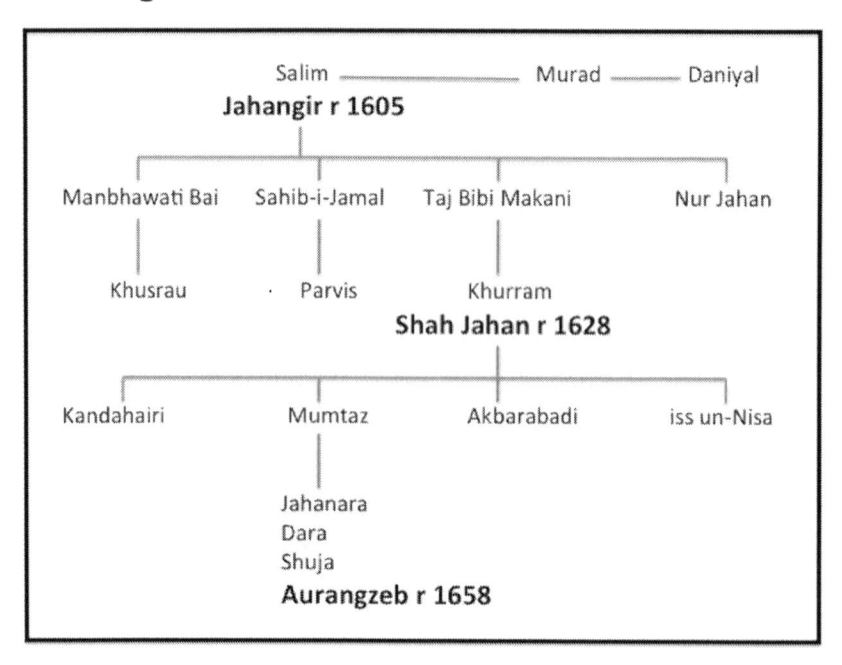

```
                    Salim ─────────── Murad ──── Daniyal
                 Jahangir r 1605
                        │
   ┌────────────┬───────┴────────┬──────────────┐
Manbhawati Bai  Sahib-i-Jamal  Taj Bibi Makani  Nur Jahan
     │              │              │
  Khusrau        Parvis          Khurram
                              Shah Jahan r 1628
                                   │
   ┌────────────┬──────────────┬──────────────┐
Kandahairi     Mumtaz         Akbarabadi     iss un-Nisa
                 │
              Jahanara
              Dara
              Shuja
             Aurangzeb r 1658
```

Shah Jahan is perhaps best known for the iconic Taj Mahal, which he commissioned in memory of his beloved wife Mumtaz Mahal. He was 15 years of age when he became engaged to Mumtaz, who was the niece of Nur Jahan. The couple married five years later, in 1612. Mumtaz was to be Shah Jahan's favourite wife and she went on to have fourteen children: eight sons and six daughters. She died at the age of 37 years, giving birth to her last child, a daughter.

At the time of Jahangir's death in 1628, the couple already had three sons: Dara Shikoh, Shah Shuja and Aurangzeb. The three princes were then living in the quarters of Nur Jahan who, according to Abdul Hamid Lahori, *'had been the cause of much strife and contention'* during the reign of Jahangir. Even more worrying was her scheming to hold onto power after the death of her husband. With Shah Jahan, the heir apparent, far away from the imperial seat at the time of the Emperor's death, the princes were in a vulnerable situation. According to Lahori, the court officials therefore decided to remove Nur Jahan from the royal palace and to put Krusau's son, Bulaki on the throne as a temporary measure until Shah Jahan was able to return to Agra and take his rightful place as the fifth Mughal Emperor.

Shah Jahan ascended the throne on the 19th January 1628. His first act was to eliminate all potential threats to his position, including his brother Shahryar and the sons of Krusrau. This included the 'temporary' throne holder, Bulaki. The sons of his brother Daniyal were also executed. Shah Jahan had ordered the execution of the unfortunate Krusrau, who had been blinded and imprisoned by his father, some six years earlier.

Military Achievements

As a royal prince and heir to the throne, Shah Jahan was given a generous *mansab* from his father, which enabled him to recruit and support his own army. In typical Mughal tradition, Jahangir sent him on various military campaigns including Mewar against the Rajputs and the Deccan against the Lodi dynasty.

In 1555, the second Mughal Emperor, Humayan, had handed Kandahar over to the Persians in exchange for military help. (Chapter Three) Several times the Mughals succeeded in retaking the city but were never able to hold on to it. In 1627, when Kandahar was once more in danger of falling to the Persians, Shah Jahan, then Prince Khurram, defied his father and refused to go to its defence. When he became Emperor, he no doubt felt some responsibility for the loss of the city. Throughout his reign he tried, unsuccessfully, to regain the Kandahar, which was both a gateway to the West and the ancestral home of the Mughals.

Shah Jahan was more successful in 1632 when the Deccan Sultanates, including the city of Golconda, submitted to Mughals rule. Some of the most valuable diamond mines were, and still are, located in the Deccan. It is thought that the famous Koh-i-Noor diamond was discovered at Golconda. (Chapter Two)

Around 1650, Shah Jahan was presented with the 'Great Mogul Diamond', which was described by the French Jeweller Tavernier, as being in the 'form of an egg cut through the middle'. The diamond fell into the hands of the Persians when Nadir Shah sacked Delhi in 1739. (Chapter Eight) Having gained the Deccan Sultanates, the Emperor appointed his third son, Aurangzeb, as Viceroy of the region.

Shah Jahan continued the work of Jahangir in strengthening and modernised his army. He encouraged the mass production of cannon at the Jaigarh Fort, which became one of the most efficient in the world and he introduced the famous Marwar horse into his cavalry. The horse is a rare breed from the Marwar region of Western Rajastan. It is a cross between an Indian pony and Arabian horse and has unusual, inward turning, ears. Known for its speed, hardiness and loyalty, it was the ideal horse for battle and was used extensively by the Mughals. The breed was still being used by the cavalry into the early 20th Century, an example being the Marwar Lancers who used the horse during the First World War.

Famine

Shah Jahan's successes coincided with a disastrous famine in the Deccan and Gujarat. A three-year drought led to starvation. According to Lahori, *'life was offered for a loaf, but none could buy; rank was sold for a cake, but none cared for it...dog's flesh was sold for goat's flesh, and the polished bones of the dead were mixed with flour and sold. Men began to devour each other, and the flesh of a son was preferred to his love.'*

Shah Jahan responded to the situation by organising soup kitchens and alms-houses across the region and he distributed money to the poor every Monday. He chose Monday because it was the day of his accession to the throne.

The Port of Hugli

In 1537, a small group of Portuguese traders settled on the right bank of the River Hugli (also spelt Hooghly), which is about 20 miles north of Calcutta. They initially erected a modest building as a trading outpost. By 1579, the settlement had grown into a township, which included a Church, known as Hugli-Chuchura. According to Lahori, some of the larger buildings were fortified with *'cannons, muskets and other implements of war'*. Over a period of time, the Europeans acquired the homes of the local people, either at a very low rent, with promise of grain, or by force. Portuguese ships began arriving at the port and eventually the local inhabitants lost trade to the foreigners, resulting in a loss of income and considerable poverty.

Mughal historians claim that some of the inhabitants became *'infected with their* [the Europeans'] *Nazarene teaching'* and were sent off in ships to Europe. Further, that *'These hateful practices were not confined to the lands they occupied, but they seized and carried off every one they could lay their hands upon along the sides of the river.'*

Shah Jahan had already heard of the situation at Hugli before he came to the throne. He blamed the problem on the local Bengali rulers who had been negligent and had failed to protect their inhabitants. He resolved to do something about it if ever he came to the throne.

Once he became Emperor, Shah Jahan appointed a new Governor of Bengal and impressed upon him the importance of *'overthrowing these mischievous people...and to set about the extermination of the pernicious intruders.'*

In 1620, Mughal forces attacked the Portuguese, both from the river and overland. Wherever possible they took the Bengali boatmen and their families to safety. According to Lahori, some four thousand boatmen, who were in the employ of the Europeans, changed sides and joined the Imperial forces.

After three and a half months, the Hugli Fort was finally bombed into submission. At this point the Portuguese and their families tried to escape by boat. One of the largest boats, carrying nearly two thousand men, women and children, plus a great deal of valuable cargo, set sail. However, fearing that the ship would fall into the hands of the Mughals, the Portuguese *'fired the magazine and blew her up'*. It is said that a statue of the Virgin Mary, rescued from the Church by the fleeing Portuguese, was lost in the river. It was later discovered on the riverbank.

By the end of the siege, almost 10,000 Portuguese had lost their lives compared with 1,000 Mughals. 4,400 Christians were taken prisoner and nearly 10,000 local Bengalis, who had been enslaved by the Portuguese, were set free. Some of the Christians were taken to Delhi where they suffered execution by being trampled to death by elephants. This was a traditional form of Mughal execution.

When Shah Jahan heard this, he ordered that all the priests be released and he granted them a piece of land on the bank of the river where they could build another Church and reinstate the lost statue of the Virgin Mary. The Church was renovated in the 1980s and was given the status of Basilica by the Vatican.

With the departure of the Portuguese, Hugli was for a short time occupied by the Dutch, who were already trading in Calcutta. In 1825, the Dutch ceded the town to the British in exchange for British possessions in Sumatra.

Mumtaz Mahal

Mumtaz Mahal was born Arjuman Banu, in Agra, on the 17th April 1593. She was of Persian nobility and followed Shi'a Islam, which was the norm for Persians at the time. Arjuman was the niece of Nur Jahan, the powerful and manipulative wife of Jahangir, mentioned in the previous chapter.

After a five-year betrothal, Arjuman was married in 1612 to Prince Khurram, the future Shah Jahan, on a date determined by the court astrologers. Arjuman was Shah Jahan's second wife out of four and was his favourite. The Emperor gave her the name Mumtaz Mahal, which means 'The Chosen, or Elect, of the Palace'.

According to court historians, Mumtaz was exceptionally beautiful and it was a very happy marriage. She accompanied the Emperor on most of his campaigns despite fourteen pregnancies over a period of nineteen years. Shah Jahan respected her wisdom and integrity and he gave her powers of authority on his behalf. Unlike her aunt, Nur Jahan, Mumtaz Mahal showed no interest in political intrigue and has been portrayed as the model wife and Empress.

In 1631, while accompanying the Emperor on campaign against rebel leader Khan Jahan Lodi, Mumtaz went into a thirty-hour labour with her fourteenth child. Despite the best efforts of the top court physicians, Mumtaz died of postpartum haemorrhage, which was exacerbated by her numerous earlier pregnancies.

Shah Jahan was distraught at the death of his beloved wife, who was just 39 years of age. He ordered a long period of state mourning and it is said that from that moment he stopped pulling out grey hairs from his hair and beard. Consequently, he appeared to go 'white overnight'. His daughter Jahanara, the first child of his marriage to Mumtaz, was a great comfort throughout his grieving and she went on to become his Chief Consort. He later took two further wives, but more for political expediency than for companionship or affection.

Taj Mahal

Mumtaz was temporarily buried in a walled garden that Daniyal, Shah Jahan's uncle, had built in the city of Burhanpur. Six months after her death, the body was disinterred and taken in a golden casket to Agra by her son Shah Shuja. It remained interred in a small building on the banks of the Yamuna River until it found its final resting place in the Taj Mahal.

Within a year of Mumtaz's death, Shah Jahan commissioned the building of a mausoleum to house his wife's tomb. He chose a site on the banks of the Yamuna River in Agra and appointed the Persian architect Ustad Ahmad Lahauri to oversee the project. Shah Jahan had been interested in architecture from a very early age and according to court historians he was closely involved in the whole project, from drawing up the initial plans, to the final decoration. The central building, which houses the tomb, took some 20,000 artisans about eleven years to complete. Later phases, including a mosque and extensive gardens, required another ten years' work.

The design of the Taj Mahal draws from both Persian and Mughal architecture with a strong Timurid influence. Whereas earlier Mughal architecture, for example Humayan's tomb, was primarily of red sandstone, the Taj Mahal was built using white marble, inlaid with semi-precious stones. In the words of Abraham Eraly:

'Cold, hard perfection was Shah Jahan's ideal, and it is cold, hard perfection that we see in his cultural expressions, especially in the Taj. Only Shah Jahan could have built the Taj. The qualities of the Taj - opulent and startlingly beautiful, and yet also austere, perfect in symmetry and balance, meticulous and painstaking in craftsmanship - are all qualities which Shah Jahan cherished in his own life.'

In 1983, the Taj Mahal was designated as a UNESCO World Heritage Site and in 2007 it was declared a winner of the 2000-2007 'New Seven Wonders of the World' initiative.

Shah Jahan commissioned many other great works of Mughal architecture, including the Red Fort and the Jama Masjid, which is one of the largest mosques in India. Most of these great buildings were constructed in an area that was known at the time as Shahjahanabad (city of Shah Jahan). Today the area is known as Old Delhi.

Another feature of Shah Jahan's reign was the famous Peacock Throne, which was inaugurated in 1635 after seven years' work. Court chroniclers Lahori and Inyat Khan, as well as the French Jeweller Tavernier give slightly differing descriptions of the throne. All agreed, however, on the extravagant use of gold, rubies, pearls and diamonds. Some said that it even cost more to create than the construction of the Taj Mahal.

In order to secure a regular supply of precious stones, Shah Jahan would send his officials across the empire in search of the best gems available. Apart from the diamond mines in the Deccan, his representatives would be at the port of Surat to meet the incoming ships with their precious cargo. It is possible that Shah Jahan was the wealthiest man in the world at the time.

Nadir Shah of Persia seized the original Peacock Throne when he sacked Delhi in 1739. A copy was later made but this disappeared at the time of the Indian Uprising in 1857.

Wars of Succession

In 1658, at the age of 66 years, Shah Jahan became ill. His eldest daughter Jahanara, who had acted as Consort since the death of her mother, nursed him back to health. Dara Shikoh, his eldest and favourite son, was also with him in the palace. It was the Emperor's decision to keep his eldest son with him in Agra, rather than to send him on campaign or award him a governorship in some distant province. This was a sure sign that Dara was the favourite to succeed.

It came as no surprise therefore, when Shah Jahan officially announced that Dara should act as Regent during the time he was indisposed. Nevertheless, his other sons were angered by the decision and in traditional Timurid fashion, each decided to challenge the decision. At the time, Shah Shuja, the second son, was Viceroy of Bengal and Murad Baksh, the youngest, was Viceroy of Gujarat.

Shuja immediately proclaimed himself Emperor and marched with his army towards Agra. But he was beaten back by the Imperial Army under the command of Dara and was forced to sign a Peace Treaty. Murad Baksh also proclaimed himself Emperor but being the least likely of the four brothers to succeed, he decided to join Aurangzeb, the third son, in the fight against Dara. Aurangzeb was by far the most able of the sons. From an early age he had excelled himself on the battlefield and had held many important positions proving him to be a good administrator.

A decisive battle between the Imperial forces under Dara and an alliance between Aurangzeb and Murad, known as the Battle of Samugarh, took place on the 29th May 1658. While Murad excelled himself on the battlefield, it was Aurangzeb who claimed victory. In defeat, Dara fled towards Agra and Aurangzeb was declared Emperor.

Despite the fact that Shah Jahan made a complete recovery, Aurangzeb declared him incompetent to rule and had him confined to Agra Fort. Jahanara remained with her father during the last sad years of his life. He was confined for eight years and died at the age of 74 years. Although father and son communicated throughout this period, Aurangzeb never visited Shah Jahan.

Jahanara had planned a State funeral for her father but Aurangzeb believed this to be too ostentatious. Instead the coffin was taken unceremoniously by river to the Taj Mahal, where his body was interred next to his beloved Mumtaz.

Conclusion

Shah Jahan's accession was surrounded by both political intrigue and violence. As was the pattern in Mughal history, the death of the Emperor usually led to a battle for succession between the surviving sons. It was also a battle between life and death, because the defeated sons inevitably faced execution as a precaution against further challenge to the throne. Shah Jahan followed the tradition and was ruthless in his elimination of his own brothers and nephews.

By the 17th Century, when Shah Jahan came to the throne, royal biographies, both commissioned and non-commissioned, were becoming commonplace. Furthermore, there were letters and eyewitness reports of the growing number of European traders, travellers and diplomats. Consequently, we have a great deal of information about Shah Jahan and his rule. The commissioned biographies, not surprisingly, portray the Emperor in a favourable light. The non-commissioned biographers were less restrained. The accounts of Europeans were often based upon court gossip and therefore less reliable. However, they provide a valuable insight into the growing Portuguese, Dutch and English communities that were beginning to settle in the Empire.

Shah Jahan is portrayed as a complex person. He appears to have been both coldly ruthless, while at the same time caring and compassionate. While brutal in his dealings with his male relatives, he showed genuine concern for the starving at the time of the Deccan famine. His dealings with the Europeans were also inconsistent. For example, he ordered the Bengali Governor to 'exterminate the pernicious intruders', but then he ordered the release of the priests and gave them land for a new Church.

He is described by Thomas Row as *'never smiling, or in face showing any respect or difference of men, but mingled with extreme pride and contempt of all.'* At the same time he was capable of maintaining stable and close relationships, not only with his wife Mumtaz Mahal, but also his daughter Jahanara and son Dara.

While Shah Jahan was unable to extend his Empire, there was considerable consolidation, which was largely due to the efforts of his son Aurangzeb. The total submission of the Deccan, with its valuable diamond mines, brought even more wealth into the royal treasury, at a time when Shah Jahan may already have been the wealthiest man in the world.

After three unsuccessful attempts to regain Kandahar the Emperor finally accepted the fact that the ancestral home of Babur, the first Mughal Emperor, was lost to the Persians.

The Emperor's final days were as full of political intrigue as his first days on the throne. His greatest legacy is undoubtedly his contribution to Mughal architecture, the most iconic being the Taj Mahal, recognised worldwide as a symbol of romantic love.

CHAPTER SEVEN

Aurangzeb the Austere

Aurangzeb, also referred to as Alamgir, is generally considered to be the last of the Great Mughals before the Empire went into steady decline. He was born *Abu'l* Muzaffar Muhl-ud-Din Muhammad, on the 3rd November 1618, in Dahod, Gujarat. He was the third out of four sons from the marriage between Shah Jahan and Mumtaz Mahal.

While Shah Jahan was probably best known for the Taj Mahal, Aurangzeb is more usually remembered for his cruel treatment of his father and his religious intolerance. An understanding of his early years, however, may go some way towards explaining his behaviour.

Apparently, Aurangzeb was a sickly child and it was clear from an early age that would never live up to his father's expectations. Dara, the eldest son, was the favourite and none of the three younger boys could compete with him for their father's love and affection. Out of the three, Aurangzeb stood out as being the most different to Dara and this became more pronounced in adulthood.

It can happen that if a younger sibling lives in the shadow of a favoured older brother or sister, he or she will become a rebel. This may well have been the case with Aurangzeb. At an early age, he displayed an inward rebellious attitude when it came to his studies. As was tradition, he commenced his studies in his fourth year on a date and at a time determined by the astrologers. Although he was a diligent student, he did not enjoy either his studies or his tutors.

He portrayed his feelings towards one of his former tutors when the latter appeared at court soon after his accession. According to Manucci, Aurangzeb angrily attacked the man with the words:

'What can I do but weep when I remember that in my tender age I fell into your hands...Forgetting how many important subjects ought to be embraced in the education of a Prince, you acted as if it were chiefly necessary that he would possess great skill in

grammar, and such knowledge as belongs to a doctor of law; and thus did you waste the precious hours of my youth in the dry, unprofitable and never-ending task of learning words!

...Was it not your duty to teach me the customs of the Mughal princes, to inform me that one day I should be forced to take the field, sword in hand, against my brothers, if not to gain a crown, at least to defend my life?

...If you did not know the military art, you might at least have taught me the methods of governing the people when my father should send me to rule some province. You might have laid down rules for the equal administration of justice, the way of capturing a people's love.'

It should be pointed out that Manucci, the Italian traveller who spent time at the Mughal court, recounted these words. As mentioned earlier, European reports regarding the inner life of the palace were often based on hearsay. Jadunath Sarkar, who wrote a *History of Aurangzib* in 1912, reminds us that Manucci was a young runaway, of poor education, who wrote his accounts long after the events. Consequently, their reliability should be treated with caution.

Despite these reservations, it is possible to detect something of Aurangzeb's childhood experience and adult views from this short passage. He clearly thought that his early education, which would have been based on the classical studies of languages, literature and the arts, was a waste of time. But perhaps more revealing is that he placed such importance on an education that would prepare him to be an efficient and just ruler. He also shows that gaining the love of his people was very important to him.

Aurangzeb's letters further reveal his desire to be loved, not only by the common people, but also by his close supporters and members of his family. This obsession was probably born out of his relationship with his father, who not only showed him no love, but also constantly criticised him, even in public.

Mancucci describes Aurangzeb as being *'very different from the others, being in character very secretive and serious, carrying on his affairs in a hidden way...He was of a melancholy temperament...wishing to execute justice and arrive at appropriate decisions. He was extremely anxious to be recognised by the world as a man of wisdom, clever and a lover of truth. He was moderately liberal...For a long time he pretended to be a faqir, a holy mendicant, by which he renounced the world, gave up all claim to the crown, and was content to pass his life in prayers and mortifications.'*

From his early life, Aurangzeb was certainly secretive and scheming. What he lacked in both physical strength and charm, he made up for in political guile and this is what eventually gave him an advantage over all his other brothers.

The Fate of the Brothers

Aurangzeb ascended the throne as the sixth Mughal Emperor on the 13th June 1659. Before this, however, he had to deal with the elimination of any threat from his brothers.

Shah Shuja, the second son, had never been a serious contender for the throne. Like many other Mughal princes before him, he was more interested in wine, women and opium, than the serious business of politics and government. Furthermore, he was a Shi'a, which by the 17th Century would have been unacceptable to the majority of the Mughal population, which at that time practised Sunni Islam. During the Wars of Succession that broke out towards the end of Shah Jahan's rule, Shuja fled to the Punjab and then to Burma, where he died in 1661.

Murad, the youngest of the four sons, was also a Shi'a. According to Manucci, *'He was a man of little wisdom, who could not plan anything beyond his amusements, drinking, singing and dancing.'* However, he was an excellent hunter and excelled on the battlefield. It was due to Murad's outstanding bravery at the Battle of Samugarh, that Aurangzeb's forces were able to defeat Dara and the Imperial army.

Aurangzeb took advantage of Murad's political incompetency. He promised Murad that if he would join forces, Aurangzeb would divide the Empire with him once they had defeated Dara. Following the victory, however, Aurangzeb reneged on his promise and secretly had Murad arrested. After three years in prison the Prince was accused of murder and sentenced to death. He died at the age of 37, on the 14th December 1661.

This leaves Dara, the eldest son, heir to the throne and Shah Jahan's favourite. According to Manucci, Dara was *'a man of dignified manners, of a comely countenance, joyous and polite in conversation, ready and gracious of speech, of most extraordinary liberality, kindly and compassionate but over-confident in his opinion of himself, considering himself competent in all things and having no need of advisers. He despised those who gave him counsel.'*

Apparently, Dara enjoyed the company of buffoons and took great delight in humiliating visitors, of the highest rank, who came to the court. He also enjoyed the company of Europeans, particularly Jesuit priests, and spent time drinking and conversing with them. In common with his great grandfather, Akbar, he spent time with Sufis, Jews, Hindus and Christians.

During Shah Jahan's illness, Dara banned all visits to the court. He assumed for himself the power of running the Empire in all but name. Rumours began to spread that the Emperor was dead, perhaps even poisoned by his favourite son. In order to reassure his subjects, Shah Jahan dragged himself to a window to show that he was still alive. However, some suspected that this was an imposter dressed in the Emperor's clothing.

Dara's childish behaviour and religious liberality angered Aurangzeb. He was himself a strict Sunni Muslim and he considered Dara, and to a lesser extent, Shuja and Murad, to be infidels because they did not live according to Islamic Law. With this conviction, he was able to legitimise his harsh treatment of his brothers and father. He believed that it was necessary to act as he did, to both ensure the survival of the Empire and save it from heresy.

Immediately after his defeat at Samugarh, Dara fled towards Agra and then on to Lahore and Sindh. He tried to raise troops among the Afghan rulers but all his efforts were thwarted. Aurangzeb, forever the political opportunist, had already formed alliances with many regional powers. Unfortunately for Dara, one such power, an Afghan chieftain, betrayed him. On the 10th June 1659, he was handed over to Aurangzeb's army, together with one of his sons.

Dara was taken to Delhi, placed on a filthy elephant and to his humiliation, was paraded through the streets in chains. Aurangzeb then called a council which judged Dara to be a political threat and also guilty of apostasy. He was executed by four of Aurangzeb's henchmen on the 30th August 1659. His severed head was taken to Aurangzeb for identification. Crowds then lined the streets of Delhi, many of them weeping, as the Prince's headless body was once more paraded through the streets. He was buried, with no ritual washing, in a vault within Humayan's tomb.

But Dara remains alive in the Indian imagination. Debates continue as to what the consequences might have been for India, should Dara have succeeded to the throne rather than Aurangzeb. In February of this year (2017), *'The Indian Express'* announced that the Indian Council of Cultural Relations was to host a seminar dedicated to Dara. Furthermore, Dalhousie Road in Delhi (named after the British Governor General), was to be renamed Dara Road.

The Enthronement

Paradoxically, the enthronement of Aurangzeb, the most austere of all Mughal Emperors, was the most magnificent. This was because he inherited the glory that Shah Jahan had created. The Peacock Throne did not exist at the time of Shah Jahan's enthronement, whereas Aurangzeb was able to take his place on this expensively jewelled throne for his ceremony. Furthermore, Aurangzeb's enthronement took place immediately after his victory in the Wars of Succession. Consequently, the occasion was as much a victory parade as it was an enthronement.

We get a very good description of the event that took place on 13th June 1659, from Judanath Sarkar's *History of Aurangzib*. He tells us that the sovereign *'mounts the throne fully dressed, with a cloth turban bound round his head. Diamonds and jewels glitter on that turban...An eloquent chanter mounted a lofty rostrum and in a clear ringing voice read the khutba or public proclamation of the Emperor's name and titles, prefaced with the praise of God and the Prophet, and followed by the names of his predecessors on the throne. As every such name fell from his lips a fresh robe of honour was bestowed on him. And when he came to the recital of the Emperor's own titles, he got a cloth of gold.'*

Aurangzeb was just over forty when he came to the throne. Unlike many Mughal Princes, who showed signs of a life of excess, Aurangzeb was slim. He was tall and had a long face. Sarkar says that under a *'broad, unwrinkled forehead beamed two cold piercing eyes, whose serenity no danger or fear could disturb, no weakness or pity relax.'*

The palace and Hall of Public Audience were richly decorated. *'The door and walls of the Hall were tapestried with embroidered velvet, flowered velvet, European screens, and gold tissue from Turkey and China'.*

The banks of the Yumna River were illuminated and the Imperial Artillery Department put on a massive firework display. The festivities continued for several weeks during which time the Emperor received a constant supply of gifts from his nobles, officers and courtiers. In return Aurangzeb gave out promotions and gifts while coins were distributed to the people.

Aurangzeb and Religion

In the tradition of their ancestor, Timur, the Mughals were nominally Sunni Muslims. Shi'a influences were strong, however, during Humayan's reign resulting from his period of exile at the Safavid court in Persia. The third Emperor, Akbar, positively encouraged religious tolerance and promoted religious equality across the Empire. While Jahangir and Shah Jahan were less tolerant of non-Muslims, this was more to do with indifference than a thought through theology.

The reign of Aurangzeb was to be markedly different and it is generally thought that his religious policies contributed to the decline of the Empire. From an early age, he was reflective and tended towards the melancholy. He was also obsessed with a sense of sin. As often happens with an unloved child, all his efforts to please his father were rejected. Consequently, he came to believe that he did not deserve his father's love because of some wrongdoing.

His actions towards father and brothers were harsh, but he believed they were justified. Nevertheless, they played on his conscience. He felt the need to somehow make recompense and the solution was to become a more devout Muslim. Aurangzeb's commitment took two forms; first in his personal life and second in his dealings with the Empire.

In his personal life, he adhered strictly to the *Sharia*, or Islamic Law. He spent many hours in prayer and memorised the Koran by heart. He lived a frugal life and wore simple clothes. From the time, he ascended the throne he showed no interest in music. The great Mughal architecture held no appeal for him and he refused to have paintings, depicting the human form, in his private quarters. He did, however, enjoy the art of calligraphy and would sell copies of his own work in order to pay for his personal expenses.

One of his first acts on becoming Emperor, and by way of remitting his sins, was to send alms to the holy city of Mecca and commission ships to carry pilgrims from India making the *Hajj*. He then began the process of enforcing *Sharia* law across the Empire according to the strict Hanafi Code. (See below)

Contrary to advice from his nobles and his sister Roshanara, to whom he was very close, Aurangzeb reintroduced the *Jizya* tax on all non-Muslims, thus undoing one of the most progressive policies of Akbar. He prohibited the building of new temples or the repair of old ones. While he undoubtedly sanctioned the destruction of some Hindu and Jain temples, opinions differ as to the extent of the destruction. Current thinking is that original accounts were exaggerated and far fewer temples were destroyed than earlier thought.

Fatawa-e-Alamgiri

Possibly Aurangzeb's greatest legacy in terms of religion was the Fataw-e-Alamgiri, which was a compilation of Islamic Law that was based on Sunni Hanafi Canon Law. The work was commissioned by Aurangzeb in order to place *Sharia* Law on a firm footing across the Empire.

Some 500 experts in Islamic jurisprudence gathered to work on the compilation. They were scholars from Medina, Baghdad, Delhi and Lahore. The work took several years to complete and formed 30 volumes.

The introduction of the Fatawa-e-Alambiri affected the lives of everyone in the Mughal Empire. Significantly, it changed a status of equality before the law to inequality. For example, Sayyids, who were Muslims claiming descent from the Prophet Muhammad, were exempt from prison sentences or any form of physical punishment, while Non-Muslims could expect the harshest of punishments for the same crime.

Apart from criminal law, the Fatawe-e-Alamgiri also covered issues of personal law relating to inheritance, apostasy, marriage and the right to own slaves. Of significant interest is that under this law, a guardian of a Muslim girl could force her to marry against her will and a Muslim man had the right to have sex with a slave girl. These latter points bring to mind the actions of the so-called Islamic State who commonly force girls into marriage and sex against their will, claiming the practice to be 'Islamic'.

Aurangzeb appointed religious police to enforce compliance, particularly when it came to the manufacture and consumption of alcohol, dress codes and sexual morality. At one point he even stipulated the length of beard that men should wear in order to comply with Islamic Law. Once more, we are reminded that the Taliban in Afghanistan and to a lesser extent in Pakistan, deploy religious police to enforce such 'morality'. On a more positive note, Aurangzeb criminalised the practise of *sati*, which actually went further than Akbar, who simply legalised the remarriage widows

The Fatawa-e-Alambiri remained in force across South Asia from the 18th to the early 20th Century. When the British came to power in the mid 19th Century they continued to use some elements of Aurangzeb's *Sharia* code where it suited their purpose.

The Rise of the Maratha Empire

Aurangzeb's policies clearly discriminated against Hindus and led to a great deal of unrest among the majority Hindu population. Even before the imposition of *Sharia* Law, however, there were constant rebellions against Mughal rule.

The greatest threat came from the Marathas, who were a group of clans living in the region of modern Maharashtra. The Marathas were renowned as fierce and fearless warriors. What they may have lacked in numbers, they made up for with their fighting skills.

In 1674, after a series of successful raids into Mughal territory, the Maratha leader Shivaji was crowned Chhatrapati (King) of the Marathas. Shivaji's mother had named him after the goddess Shivai, and like his mother, he was deeply religious. From an early age, he studied the great Hindu epics Ramayana and Mahabharata, both of which were to influence his religiosity and underpin his political thought.

During his reign, Shivaji promoted Marathi and Sanskrit rather than Persian, which was the court language of the Mughals. But he is best known for introducing the concept of *Hindavi Swarajya,* which broadly means Hindu Self-Rule. In the 17th Century, this meant a fight for self-rule against the Mughals. In the 19th and 20th Centuries, Indian leaders promoted *Hindavi Swarajya* in the fight for self-rule against the British.

Shivaji's successors were to continue the fight against the Mughals. The conflict, known as the Mughal-Maratha wars, lasted from 1680 until 1707. At the time of Aurangzeb's death, Queen Tarabai, who was acting as regent for her son, Shivaji II, ruled the Marathas. In true Maratha fashion, she did not simply rule in name, but led her forces in the field.

Following the death of Aurangzeb, the Marathas continued their expansion northwards, at the expense of the Mughals, until their Empire replaced the Mughals as the major power in the Indian sub-continent.

The East India Company

The East India Company's presence in India goes back to 1612 when King James I sent Sir Thomas Roe (Chapter Five) to the Mughal Court requesting trading rights. In 1619, Emperor Jahangir granted the Company rights to trade at the port of Surat. At that time the Portuguese, Dutch, Danes and French were also competing for trade in the Empire, but the English appeared to be the favoured power and eventually became the major traders

When Aurangzeb came to the throne, the Company was operating no less than 23 factories, the main ones being Fort William in Bengal, Fort St George in Madras and Bombay Castle. The Portuguese, being the first Europeans to settle in India, already held settlements along the coast of Gujarat. Bombay was transferred to of the English in 1661, as part of Catherine of Braganza's dowry when she married Charles II of England. In 1668, the English Government leased the islands to the East India Company for an annual payment of £10.

Relations between the Mughals and the East India Company did not always run smoothly. In 1682, the Company sent William Hedges to Bengal to ask the Mughal Governor for permission to trade on a regular basis throughout the Mughal Empire. The Governor of the Company at the time was Sir Josiah Child who was often criticised for running the Company as if it was his own private business. True to form, he interfered with the delicate negotiations that were taking place in Bengal. This angered Aurangzeb and the relationship between the Mughals and the East India Company completely broke down, leading to what became known as Child's War.

Ships were sent out from England and for four years, between 1686 and 1690, the Mughals and the East India Company were in armed conflict. Eventually the English were forced to concede defeat. Company representatives were sent to Aurangzeb to seek his pardon. They were forced to prostrate before the Emperor and promise to behave better in the future. After receiving a large indemnity, Aurangzeb agreed to withdraw his troops. He then permitted the Company to re-establish itself in Bombay and also set up new base in Calcutta.

At about the same time, English pirates operating out of Bombay were seizing ships taking pilgrims to Mecca, including a ship owned by the Emperor. To add to Aurangzeb's anger, the English were also minting coins with a superscription containing the English king's name. In response, Aurangzeb seized the factory at Surat and expelled all the English from his Empire. After paying a huge levy, they were allowed to return and for the next fifty years there were no further attempts to usurp power.

The Final Years

Aurangzeb died of natural causes in March 1707 at the age of 89 years. He was the longest ruling of all the Mughal Emperors and during his reign the Empire reached its greatest territorial expansion. To the very end, despite his age and fragility, he led his armies from the front in his on-going battle with the Marathas.

Although Aurangzeb survived some of his own children, he still left behind a significant number of sons and grandsons, all of whom could potentially challenge the succession. He attempted to avoid the usual wars of succession by sending his sons off to different parts of the Empire and he even considered dividing his territories in the same way that Genghis Khan had done in the 13th Century. His hopes for a peaceful succession were to be dashed.

The heir apparent, Muhammad Azam Shah, ascended the throne in March 1707. But true to Timurid fashion, a stepbrother, Muhammad Alam Shah, killed him along with his family just a few months later. Alam Shah then ascended the Mughal throne, as Bahadur Shah I, on the 19th June 1707. But the days of the Great Mughal were over and the Empire went into steady decline. By 1758, just fifty years after the death of Aurangzeb, the Mughal House of Timur was left with control of an area little more than Delhi and its environs.

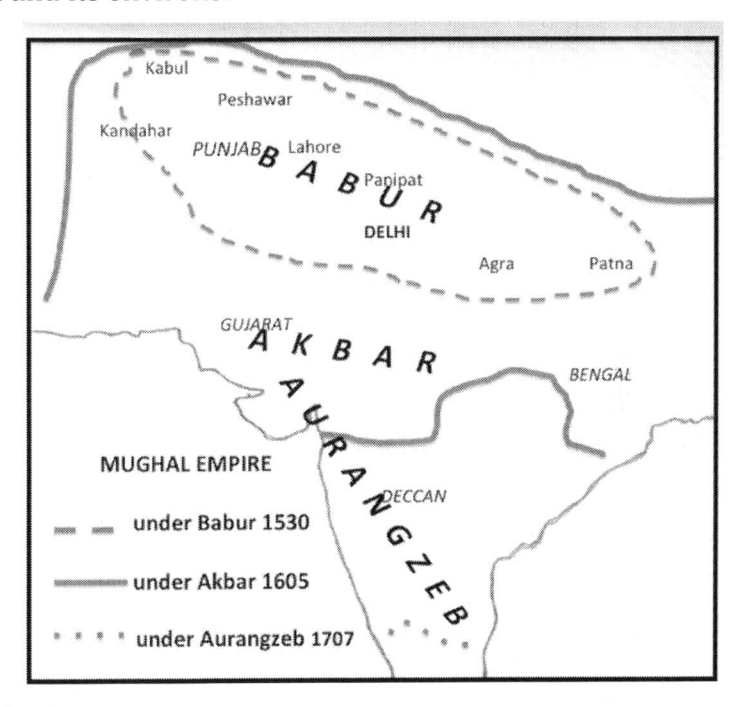

Conclusion

Aurangzeb is probably the most controversial of all the Mughal Emperors. He is also the one who has been the most severely judged by history. But this may be doing him an injustice.

Soon after he came to the throne, Aurangzeb dismissed the court chroniclers and so there is no equivalent to the *Akbarnama* or *Jahangirnama,* works that were commissioned with the sole purpose of portraying the Emperor in a good light. With Aurangzeb, we are left with non-commissioned works and his own letters, only a few of which have been published, out of five thousand that are extant.

As more of these documents are coming to light, and especially his letters, the man behind the austere face is being revealed as someone who was deeply committed to his duty as Emperor and guardian of the people.

He ruled for fifty years, longer than any other Mughal Emperor. This would not have been possible without a firm hand. Whenever it was necessary to act in a ruthless, perhaps even cruel way, he had to convince himself that his action was justified. But he was able to 'forgive and forget', an example being when he allowed the East India Company to return to Bombay.

Aurangzeb's religious policies raise several questions. For example, was his re-imposition of the *jijya* tax simply aimed at raising badly needed income? His constant military campaigns were draining the treasury and the new taxes would certainly help. On the other hand, being such a devout Muslim, he sincerely hoped for the conversion of Hindus to Islam and the hardship imposed by the tax may have encouraged them to convert. Indeed, Aurangzeb rewarded those who did convert with gifts and lucrative positions.

Aurangzeb's decision to introduce the *Sharia* Law has been highly criticised and it is often suggested that this was the reason for the decline of the Empire. But this is to ignore other elements that need to be taken into account. First, his life-long obsession with expansion that was damaging and unsustainable. Second was the increasing aggression and power of the Marathas. Third was the growing presence and influence of the English East India Company. Aurangzeb could have curtailed his expansionist policies, but the situation with the Marathas and East India Company was beyond his control.

However, one may speculate about the reign of Aurangzeb, the man behind the throne comes through in his letters, such as the following, which was written to his sons just before he died:

'This weak old man, this shrunken, helpless creature, is afflicted with a hundred maladies ...I do not know who I am, where I am, where I am to go and what will happen to a sinful person like me.'

CHAPTER EIGHT

The Last Emperor

Aurangzeb, the sixth Mughal Emperor, was the last in a line of great Emperors, each one being 'great' for a different reason. None of his successors, however, was able to reverse the steady decline that began in 1707 and ended with the dissolution of the Empire in 1858.

As the central power of the Mughals weakened, a process of fragmentation began. Local rulers withdrew their allegiance to either the Mughal Emperor or Maratha Empire and operated as minor Islamic sultanates or small Hindu kingdoms, very often competing against each other. It was in this climate of instability, with small independent states in open conflict, that the East India Company formed its own armed force, ostensibly in order to protect its trade.

At the same time the Mughals faced the growing power of the Marathas and the aggressive actions of the East India Company. In 1739, the Mughals faced their greatest challenge yet, this time from the Persians.

Nadir Shah

Nadir Shah was born in 1688, into a semi-nomadic tribe of Khorasan, which was then part of Persia. His father, who was a simple herder, died when he was 13years. Holding Genghis Khan up as his role model, he quickly learned how to support himself in a hostile environment. At that time, the Safavids, who ruled Persia, were in a weak position as a result of on-going wars with both the Ottomans and Russians. By 1736, Nadir Shah had enough support to take advantage of the situation and his armies overthrew Abbas III, marking the end of the Safavid dynasty. Nadir Shah then assumed power and became Shah of Persia.

Two years later he turned his attention towards Mughal India. After conquering Kandahar in 1738, Nadir Shah swept through the Khyber Pass with his cavalry of 150,000 and easily defeated a Mughal army numbering around 1.5 million.

His next move was towards Delhi, seat of the Mughal throne. He managed to capture the Mughal Emperor, Muhammad Shah, and march him through the streets of Delhi. A skirmish broke out resulting in several Persian soldiers being killed. In his anger, Nadir Shah ordered the sacking of the city.

Between 20,000 and 30,000 Indians were killed by the Persians in the course of one day. The carnage finally stopped when Muhammad Shah handed over the keys to the royal treasury, enabling Nadir Shah to take his pick from treasure that had been amassed by the Mughals over some two hundred years.

It is estimated that 700 elephants, 4,000 camels and 12,000 horses transported gold, silver and precious stones, valued at some £87m in the currency of the time, back to Persia. The most valuable items to be taken were the Peacock Throne, which had been commissioned by Shah Jahan, the Koh-i-Noor diamond that had been seized by Babur and the Darya Nur diamond.

The sack of Delhi by the Persians and seizure of so much treasure and gold, crippled the finances of the Mughals, which further exacerbated an already crumbling Empire.

The Carnatic Wars

Europeans had been trading with India since the early 16th Century, each one with its own 'East India Company': The Portuguese (1500), English (1600), Dutch (1602) and Danish (1616). After the Act of Union in 1707, which united England and Scotland, the 'English East India Company' officially became the 'British East India Company'. However, since the British eventually became the predominant European power in India, the title 'East India Company', 'EIC', or simply 'The Company', is usually understood to refer to the British East India Company.

The last European power to arrive in India was the French, who founded the French East India Company in 1664 in direct competition with the English. Their main trading posts were along the South-Eastern coast of the peninsula, with their capital at Pondicherry.

By the middle of the 18th Century, the Carnatic region, approximately today's Tamil Nadu, Karnataka, Kerala and southern Andhra Pradesh, came under the rule of Nizam-ul-Mulk of Hyderabad. During the early period of his early reign he was loyal to Aurangzeb, but following the latter's death in 1707, he broke away and ruled the Carnatic region as an independent entity.

When Nizam-ul-Mulk died in 1748, there followed the inevitable struggle for succession. The ensuing chaos gave both the British and the French an opportunity to interfere in Indian affairs. The British supported Nasir Jung, the Nizam's son, while the French supported Muzaffar Jung, who was the Nizam's grandson.

A similar situation occurred with the death of Dost Ali Khan, the Nawab of Arcot, who died in 1749. Dost Ali was officially a vassal of the Nizam of Hyderabad, but in reality, he ruled autonomously. When Dost Ali died, the French supported his son-in-law Chanda Sahib and the British supported the Nawab's son, Muhammad Ali.

Just as an aside, the world 'Nawab' became 'Nabob' under the British. It was then shortened to the word 'nob', and later crept into the English language, signifying a person of wealth and high social position. This is just one example of the many hundreds of words that have found their way into the English language as a result of the British presence in India.

The conflicts between the British and French during the 18th Century, lasted from 1744 to 1763. There were three separate wars, known as the 'Carnatic Wars'. These were an extension of the European Wars, for example the War of Austrian Succession, that were being waged in Europe at the time.

Clive of India

The Carnatic wars marked a change in the balance of power in India. Already weakened from the invasion of Nadir Shah and the growing number of regional rulers who were declaring 'independence' from the Emperor, the Mughals did not have the military resources to fight back.

In the middle of the 18th Century, the British were master of the seas and were gradually eliminating all rivals. By 1763, the British had also managed to defeat the French in India. This left them with almost total control of most of the sub-continent. It would then be a short step to establishing the British Raj.

Much credit for the British success at this time was given to Major-General Robert Clive, also known as Clive of India, Commander-in-Chief of British India. From an early age, Clive was known to rebel against authority and get into scrapes. His father passed him from one school to another in the hope that he would settle down and study. In 1744, having shown no academic promise, his father secured him a position with the East India Company as a 'factor', or Company agent.

During the First Carnatic War, despite the fact that it was a downward step, or that he had no military training, Clive moved from a clerical post to join the Company army. He excelled himself in the fight against the French and was given a commission as ensign. In 1751, with a small contingency of men, he successfully defended Arcot against the French. By now his name was becoming famous in England and Prime Minister William Pitt the Elder described Clive as a 'heaven-born general' despite the fact that he had no formal military training.

In 1756, Siraj Ud Daulah, the Nawab of Bengal, attacked the English settlement and fort at Calcutta, resulting in a financial loss to Company investors, estimated at £2,000,000. At the same time, British men, women and children were imprisoned in a small cell. Crammed together and in the stifling heat, 123 out of the original 146 prisoners died. The incident became famous and is known as 'The Black Hole of Calcutta'.

In order to reverse the situation, Clive came to a 'gentleman's agreement' with Mir Jaffa, Commander-in-Chief to the Nawab. If Mir Jaffa agreed to rebel against his ruler, Clive promised to make him Nawab of Bengal in his place. In return, Mir Jaffa agreed to pay a million pounds in sterling to the Company in reparations for the damage done to British property in Calcutta, half a million pounds to the British residents of Calcutta, with further amounts payable to native residents and Armenian merchants. This is an example of the many 'deals' arranged by Clive, which in time bled the Indians of their wealth and put huge profits into the Company's treasury.

The conflict between the Nawab of Bengal and the British came to a head in 1757 at the Battle of Plassey. The British defeated the Bengali forces and the Nawab was executed. This left the way clear for the implementation of the 'gentleman's agreement', whereby Mir Jaffa succeeded as Nawab. Apart from monies already agreed upon, Clive received a personal payment of £160,000, which was a vast fortune for the time.

The Company was already exempt from Customs duties under a *Firman* granted in 1717. In August 1765, Clive secured from the Mughal Emperor another *Firman* granting the Company the titles of Bengal, Bihar and the Deccan. Under this new arrangement, the Company received the right to collect taxes on behalf of the Emperor. This led to corruption and aggressive heavy handedness by Company agents. Furthermore, the Company was accused of doing nothing to alleviate the suffering of the people when a serious famine broke out in the years 1769-1770, which cost the lives of almost a third of the population.

When the news of these events reached London, Shareholders in the Company accused Clive of mismanagement. The issue was raised in the British Parliament by Lord North and led to the passing of the Regulating Act of 1773. The Act granted Parliament greater control of Indian affairs under the oversight of a Governor-General. The first to be appointed to the position was Warren Hastings.

Clive left India in 1767. He died in November 1774 at the age of 49 under mysterious circumstances. While no foul play was suspected, it was thought that he either took his own life or suffered a heart attack brought on by an overdose of drugs.

The Evangelicals

During the first hundred and fifty years of European presence in India, relations between Christians, Hindus and Muslims were generally very good. It was not uncommon, for example, for officers of the East India Company to take Hindu or Muslim wives, known as *bibis*, with whom they fathered numerous children. Some of these children were sent to England for their education and most enjoyed equal inheritance rights to children of their English wives. As vividly described in William Dalrymple's *White Mughals*, it was not unusual for European husbands to have several wives and concubines, dress in Indian style, eat Indian food and speak Urdu and Persian.

From the middle of the 18th Century, things began to change. Having subdued all her main rivals; Bengal in 1757, the French in 1761, Mysore in 1799 and the Marathas in 1819, Britain was becoming increasingly confident. The French were decisively beaten in 1815 at the Battle of Waterloo. The Sikhs were conquered in 1849, resulting in the famous Koh-i-Noor diamond, which they had earlier acquired from the Persians, being handed over to the British.

All this led to a sense of invincibility on the part of the British, which was manifested in a superior attitude towards the Indians and an imperial arrogance. Thomas Babington Macaulay (1800-1859), British historian and Whig politician, famously said:

'*a single shelf of a good European library was worth the whole native literature of India and Arabia.*'

He further stated that '*the historical information which has been collected from all the books written in the Sanscrit language is less valuable than what may be found in the most paltry abridgments used at preparatory schools in England...The languages of Western Europe civilized Russia. I cannot doubt that they will do for the Hindoo what they have done for the Tartar.*'

This arrogance was partly due to the rise of the Evangelicalism. The Clapham Sect, in particular, was both influential and powerful. Based in Clapham, London, they were a group of social reformers bound together by shared moral and spiritual values. Their numbers included senior Anglican Clergy and Members of Parliament.

William Wilberforce, who was central in the campaign to abolish the slave trade, was a key member of the group. However, the primary aim of the Clapham Sect was to spread the Gospel and support missionary work, not only at home, but also across the growing Empire. With this in mind, the group founded the British and Foreign Bible Society, and the Church Missionary Society, among others.

Under the Founding Charter of the East India Company, evangelising had been strictly forbidden. This no doubt contributed to the earlier good relations between European Christians and the local population. However, with the rise of Evangelicalism in the second half of the 18th Century and a powerful lobby of Evangelicals, including members of the Clapham Sect, in Parliament, the earlier ruling was overturned. India was now a target for open evangelism with the overt aim of conversion. Hymns written at the time reflect this missionary zeal. William Dalrymple, in his book *The Last Mughal*, cites the hymn written by Bishop Reginald Heber, Bishop of Calcutta, as an example:

From Greenland's icy mountains,
From India's coral strand
They call us to deliver
Their land from error's chain

In vain with lavish kindness
The gifts of God are strewn;
The heathen in his blindness
Bows down to wood and stone

The first Anglican Chaplain to the Delhi Court was the Reverend Midgeley John Jennings. Described by Dalrymple as having '*a brash and insensitive yet silkily unctuous manner - strikingly similar to that of Obadiah Slope in the Barchester Towers.* He was generally disliked but this did not stop him from going about his task with a righteous and confident zeal.

Jennings' task was made easier when the British permitted the evangelisation of children in Government orphanages and inmates in Company prisons. Occasionally, land was taken from mosques and temples and handed over to missionaries so that they could build churches.

In 1837, the British abolished Persian in favour of English as the language of Government. Over time, many in the Hindu and Muslim population came to suspect, with some justification, that the British planned to covert the whole of India to Christianity. In this context, there grew a rise in Islamic fundamentalism in reaction to what was perceived to be an aggressive Christian fundamentalism.

Bahadur Shah II, (Zafar) the Last Emperor

When Bahadur Shah II, popularly known as Zafar, was crowned as the nineteenth Mughal Emperor, on the 29th September 1837, he was described as:

His Divine Highness, Caliph of the Age, Padshah as Glorious as Jamshed, He who is Surrounded by Hosts of Angels, Shadow of God, Refuge of Islam, Protector of the Mohammedan Religion, Offspring of the House of Timur, Greatest Emperor, Mightiest King of Kings, Emperor son of Emperor, Sultan son of Sultan.

In common with many of his predecessors, Zafar was an accomplished poet and calligrapher. Being a devout Sufi, he was tolerant towards other religions.

The Mughal Empire that Zafar came to inherit was nothing more than the city of Delhi. It was a small island struggling to survive in the midst of a vast sea of vassal states belonging to the East India Company. The Company had previously been given responsibility for collecting taxes and revenue from the Mughal vassal states on behalf of the Emperor. In theory, the net proceeds should have gone to Zafar, but in practice most of the revenue went into the Treasury of the Company and the Emperor received a small personal pension as well as an allowance to cover the palace expenses.

Within his limited resources, Zafar was able to cover the expenses of his immediate family, but for the vast number of junior princes and princesses and grandchildren of previous monarchs, life was miserable. Living in poverty, they were confined to a small walled area within the palace. One British observer said that the relatives, known as *salatin*, lived in mud huts and when the gates to the quarter were opened *'there was a rush of miserable, half naked, scared being*s ...Some men 'appar*ently nearly 80 years old were almost in a state of nature'.*

While the Mughal Empire was fast coming to the end of its life, the British Government and Directors of the East India Company were making plans for the future. Zafar's own choice to succeed was Prince Jawan Bakht. Although only eight years old, and the youngest of his fifteen sons, Zafar was put under great pressure by the boy's mother Zinat Mahal, to appoint him as heir apparent. Looking back at Mughal history, it was highly unlikely that the boy would have succeeded in ascending the throne with so many brothers likely to challenge him.

The British, on the other hand, favoured the rule of primogeniture, which would make Prince Fakru, the eldest surviving son, heir apparent. Despite Zafar's wishes, secret negotiations took place between Prince Fakru, who was angered by his father's decision, and the British. In January 1852, Fakru signed a secret document whereby the British would recognise him as heir apparent on condition that once on the throne he would move the Mughal Court from the Red Fort to the suburb of Mehruli. Furthermore, he agreed to give up his superior status as Emperor and be of equal status with the British Governor General. The British plan was to remove the Emperor from the Fort, which they would then use as a military barrack.

The Indian Uprising

Things came to a head in 1857 with the Indian Uprising, also known as the Indian Mutiny, Great Rebellion, Sepoy Mutiny or India's First War of Independence. The conflict lasted from May 1857 to July 1859 and resulted in the dissolution of the Mughal Empire, the dissolution of the East India Company and the establishment of the British Raj with Queen Victoria as Sovereign.

There were a number of reasons for the outbreak of the uprising, including general unrest among the civilian population and the growing gap in the British army between British officers and native troops, known as sepoys. High caste Hindus also had concerns that due to new regulations, their particular dietary and ritual needs were under threat.

The spark that ignited the flame was a small incident relating to the introduction of a new model of rifle, the Enfield P-53. The new rifle used paper cartridges that were pre-greased. Before being inserted into the barrel, it was necessary for the sepoy to bite the end of the cartridge in order to release the powder. Rumours began to spread that the grease was made of beef and pork fat. Since Hindus are forbidden to eat beef, and Muslims forbidden to eat pork, there was outrage in the ranks. For many it was seen as an insult to their religion and further proof that the British intended to convert the Indians to Christianity.

On the 29th March 1857, Mangal Pandey, of the 34th Bengal Native Infantry, shot and injured a British Officer. When the British General ordered the Indian commander, Jemadar Prasad, to arrest Pandey, he refused. All the other sepoys present also refused to move against Pandey. Only one sepoy obeyed, an act for which he was later promoted. Both Mangal Pandey and Jemadar Prasad were executed and the regiment was disbanded and stripped of its uniforms. When news of the event spread to other regiments, sepoys began to turn against their British Officers.

Rebellions broke out amongst troops right across large parts of Northern India and in many places there were civilian riots. Atrocities occurred on both sides and the total death toll among the Indians, at the end of two years of conflict, numbered some 100,000.

As the uprising gained momentum, anti-British feeling grew. Many now looked to the Mughal Emperor, who was seen as the legitimate ruler, for leadership. Zafar was an old, disillusioned man who simply wanted a quiet life with his garden and books for company. He had no interest in politics or military affairs but pressure was put upon him to support the uprising, if only in name.

Arrest and Exile

The rebellion was finally put down on the 8th July 1859. Apart from the huge loss of life, the city of Delhi was virtually destroyed. Two thirds of the population had fled, leaving the streets deserted and in ruins. Looting was widespread, so much so that Lieutenant Ommaney commented *'Even when Nadir Shah conquered the city, this was not the case'*.

Zafar and his family had managed to escape to Humayan's tomb but it was not long before the British arrested him. He was taken back to Delhi on a palanquin and people simply stared at the old man, who looked worried and anxious, as he passed through the streets. Shortly after, the three princes, Mughal, Khizr Sultan and Abu Bakr, who had all been hiding with the Emperor at Humayan's tomb, were also arrested. They were taken a short distance by cart, ordered to get out and told to strip naked. They were then shot dead in cold blood.

Zafar was imprisoned with his family while he awaited trial for the crime of inciting mutiny. A visitor described his prison as *'a small, dirty, low room...on a low charpoy cowered a thin, small old man, dressed in a dirty white suit of cotton, and rolled in shabby wraps.'*

The last Mughal Emperor was found guilty on four counts. He was sent into exile with his wife Zinat Mahal and a few other members of the family, to Rangoon. He died on the 7th November 1862 at the age of 87 and was buried unceremoniously in an unmarked grave. His crown is now part of the British Royal Collection.

Conclusion

The 18th Century witnessed a marked change in the balance of power in India. As the Mughal Empire continued to fragment, the East India Company gained both politically and economically. It was during this time that the Company's headquarters in London permitted the recruitment armed forces. This was ostensibly to ensure the security of British trade, property and people resdent in India. In time, the Company army became a powerful war machine numbering some 200,000 troops.

A further blow for the Mughals was the invasion, in 1739, of Nadir Shah of Persia. Not only did the invasion cause financial loss, but it also damaged Mughal confidence.

Both Britain and France interfered in Indian politics. When battles for succession broke out in the case of both Nizam-ul-Mulk of Hyderabad and the Nawab of Arcot, the British and French supported different sides and armed combat broke out between the two European powers. Known as the Carnatic Wars, in reality they reflected the conflicts happening at the time in Europe.

Another example of British interference in Indian politics, was the secret agreement made with Prince Fakru, whereby Fakru promised to move the Mughal Court from the Red Fort in exchange for British help in securing the throne. This also indicates that the British were planning for the downfall of the Emperor long before it happened.

A marked change in Indian-British relations occurred with the rise of the Evangelical movement in England. Powerful voices, including members of the Clapham Sect, spoke out in Parliament for the right to evangelise India. It was an opinion supported by the public and needs to be seen in the context of Britain's growing confidence and sense of invincibility. Leading Evangelicals spoke of Britain's providence and her Christian duty to convert the heathen.

There were many reasons for the outbreak of the Indian Uprising in 1857. It was not a uniform event, but made up of numerous rebellions, large and small, across various parts of Northern and Central India. Underlying all the unrest, however, was a deep suspicion, and fear, that the British intended to convert India to Christianity. Whether or not this was the intention, or indeed even possible, it was sufficient to push many to turn against British rule.

There were atrocities committed on both sides, but as happened in the various Balkan Wars of the 19th Century, the power of the British press ensured that the enemy, whether Ottoman or Mughal, was portrayed as a barbaric heathen. Interestingly, both Ottoman and Mughal were Muslim Empires and the antipathy towards Muslim powers continues to this day.

Zafar was the *Caliph of the Age, Refuge of Islam* and *Protector of the Mohammedan Religion.* He was personally a devout Muslim. He was also a descendent of the great Timur and head of the Timurid Dynasty. It is highly unlikely that at 82 years old, the mild-mannered Emperor was involved in the plot against the British. But he was of great symbolic importance and because of this, he was removed from the throne, he was personally humiliated and he spent his final years in exile. His death five years later marked the end of the Mughal Empire.

CONCLUSION

The Mughal Empire was ruled by a dynasty that began in 1370 with the reign of the Turko-Mongol warlord Timur. Although the Empire was dissolved following the Indian Uprising in 1857, the dynasty continued through the surviving sons who managed to escape arrest by the British.

Over a period of almost five hundred years, the Timurid rulers changed from tough nomadic warlords to cultured but effete monarchs. Between these two extremes were Emperors such as Babur, Akbar and Aurangzeb who were great patrons of the arts but at the same time excelled as military leaders. Throughout the five hundred years of transition from nomad to sophisticated monarch, the Mughal aristocracy remained proud of their Timurid ancestry and looked back to Genghis and Timur as role models.

Until the rule of Aurangzeb, in the late 17th Century, all the Emperors were generally open and tolerant towards Hindus and other non-Muslims. They were also pragmatic and these two factors contributed to the success with which they were able to expand and consolidate their Empire. For example, by taking Hindu wives, the Mughals were able to secure beneficial alliances with potential enemies. It was common practice, for example, for marriages to be contracted with princesses of the warlike Hindu Rajputs, who were the Mughal's greatest threat in the 16th and 17th Centuries. In time, Rajput units joined the Mughal armies, which was a strategy that had been used by the early Timurids.

Two other examples of Mughal pragmatism occurred while Humayan was in exile in Persia. In order to secure the help of the Persians in regaining his throne, he agreed to convert to Shi'a Islam. Consequently, while Shi'a Islam remained a minority influence in the Mughal court, it never became the dominant form of Islam throughout the Empire, which remained Sunni. The other example of Humayan's pragmatism was his agreement to hand over Kandahar to the Persians. This act was to be a running sore for most of Mughal history and the city was fought over for many centuries.

Akbar's religious policies were no doubt formed for pragmatic reasons also. He knew that stable relations between the different religious and ethnic groups were essential for a stable empire. Furthermore, his overtures towards the Jesuits in Goa would have been motivated by his need for information about them, as much as his interest in Christianity.

The religious tolerance of the first five Emperors enabled stability and growth. Aurangzeb's Islamic conservatism and particularly his introduction of *Sharia* Law alienated the majority of the Hindu population and was one factor that led to the slow decline of the Empire.

In military terms, the Mughals were the dominant power in the peninsula from the reign of Akbar to Aurangzeb, largely because they acquired both firearms and expertise from the Persians, Portuguese and Ottomans. The Mughals also had a good military structure, which was based on the Mongol practice of Central Asia and later developed by Akbar. By the 18th Century, when the Empire began to fragment, the Mughals lost a source of manpower and income from taxation, both of which weakened their military capabilities.

A recurring theme that was evident from the reign of Timur to Zafar, was the problem of succession, a situation that was aggravated by the fact that all the rulers had multiple wives and numerous sons. Traditionally the sons born to the first wife or consort would take priority. It was then normal for the Emperor to nominate an heir who was not necessarily the eldest son. Not surprisingly the arrangement was bound to cause conflict and anxiety when it became clear that the Emperor was nearing the end of his life. Aurangzeb in particular expressed his concerns in his letters over the prospect of a war of succession following his death.

Another recurring theme was the dominance of powerful women that can be traced back to Genghis Khan whose mother, Hoelun, was such a significant influence in his life. Aisan Daulat Begum,

Babur's grandmother, played a similar role. In fact, it was due to her encouragement and support that he was not only able to survive an early exile and destitution, but to go on and build an Empire.

Humayan's sister, the aunt of Akbar, was extremely important in a different way. Because Akbar was illiterate and she was highly educated, she was asked to write a biography of Humayan, which became known as the *Humayan-nama*. In court life there were many powerful, but also domineering women. They could be manipulative and scheming in their ambition to get their own son on the throne. Nur Jahan, favourite wife of Jahangir, perhaps stands out as the most politically ambitious of all.

On the battlefield, women could be as fearless as any man. Rani Durgavati, the Rajput Queen of Gondwara, led her forces, mounted on a war elephant, against Akbar's Imperial army, as did Chand Bibi, Regent Queen of Akmadnagar. And Queen Tarabai led the Marathas against Aurangzeb.

Aurangzeb was probably the most unpopular Emperor, largely on account of his extreme religious policies. When he died at the age of 88 years, the Empire was at its greatest territorial extent, but it was also beginning to fragment and finances were low.

The comparative ease with which the East India Company was able to seize power was partly due to the increasing weakness of the Emperors. However, their task was also made easier because so many small Sultanates and Kingdoms were prepared to collaborate with the British in exchange for favours and protection. Although duplicity and secret deals were not the monopoly of one particular group, the British seem to have been particularly guilty in their wish to destroy the Empire and its symbol of power.

All sides in the various conflicts can be accused of brutality and atrocities. Some of the practices of the early Timurids, for example, seem to the Western reader as particularly horrific. However, considering the period of history, they were hardly more barbaric than what was happening in Europe at the time. The brutality of the Indian Uprising is especially controversial.

Each side has its own story. Until recently, British accounts have been the most widely read. Now it is possible to read Indian eyewitness accounts that have been stored in various Indian archives and only just coming to light.

The great tragedy is that so much of the Mughal legacy, particularly the great works of architecture, are now all but lost. As Dalrymple describes the Delhi of today: *'Crumbling tomb towers, old mosques or ancient colleges intrude in the most unlikely places, appearing suddenly on roundabouts or in municipal gardens, diverting the road network and obscuring the fairways of the golf course'.*

The Taj Mahal and Humayan's tomb have been preserved for the tourist. But how many of them are aware of the once magnificent Mughal Empire?

*****

EPILOGUE

The dissolution of the Mughal Empire in 1857 marked the beginning of British rule referred to as the British Raj. On the 28th June 1858, governance was transferred from the British East India Company to the British Crown. Queen Victoria became Empress of India and the subcontinent was ruled on her behalf by a Viceroy or Governor General. Indians ruled a number of autonomous Princely states, for example Hyderabad and Kashmir, under the suzerainty of the British Crown.

Just fifty years later, three other Empires were dissolved: the Ottoman Empire, the Russian Empire and the Austria-Hungarian Empire. In each case, the Emperor concerned either suffered exile or, in the case of the Russians, execution.

The Raj lasted until 1947, when India was granted Independence. Between 1857 and 1947, the British introduced new legislation and many reforms aimed at improving the penal code, health care and the education system. While much of the population benefitted, women often found themselves disadvantaged. For example, the new legislation only recognised the rights of one wife, a situation that could leave other wives and their children disadvantaged or destitute.

After seventy years of independence and with the benefit of hindsight, British and Indian historians are now looking back to those crucial years with a critical eye. Not surprisingly, opinions differ as to whether or not the Raj was a good thing for India. With the growth in recent decades of Indian nationalism, some Indians believe that despite the benefits, British rule had a negative affect on Indian culture and her sense of identity.

There is a view among the British, however, that the Raj was entirely beneficial to the Indian people. Many of those who voted in the 2016 Referendum, to leave the European Union, would probably endorse that opinion. Such individuals have been tempted by the idea that Britain can be 'great' again, that she can somehow return to those glorious days when Britain ruled the waves and a great British Empire.

At the time of writing, Philip Hammond, the British Chancellor, is visiting India. In his efforts to negotiate future trade deals, post the British decision the leave the European Union, he is appealing to the shared history that Britain and India enjoy. In reference to the period of the Raj, an Indian commentator made the point that most Indians look back to the Raj with a sense of shame.

What was a shameful episode in British-Indian relations was the disaster that followed the decision to partition India in 1947 as part of the Indian Independence Act. The Act provided for the creation of two separate countries: India, which would be predominantly Hindu and Pakistan, which would be predominantly Muslim. The partition resulted in between ten and twelve million people being displaced along religious lines. Up to two million refugees were left homeless and inter-religious violence was widespread. The recent film *Viceroy's House* attempts to capture the plight of the displaced and the hatred that erupted among people who for centuries had lived in relative peace.

The Mughals ruled for some three hundred years. British direct rule lasted for ninety years. Both powers have left their legacy. But as India now takes her place on the world stage as a major power, that legacy is becoming less significant. Today's India is confident about her identity and the Indian people are rightly proud of their Hindu roots. The challenge is to hold onto those values without undermining or excluding the other. The hope is that India's tradition of religious tolerance that lasted for centuries, will survive the current trend of a growing intolerance and nationalism that is spreading across the globe.

*****

TIMELINE

1206-1227	Reign of Genghis Khan
1370-1405	Reign of Timur
1526	First Battle of Pannipat
1526-1530	Reign of Babur, first Mughal Emperor
1530-1540	Reign of Humayun, second Mughal Emperor
1540-1555	Reign of Sher Shah Suri
1555-1556	Reign of Humayun
1556-1605	Reign of Akbar, third Mughal Emperor
1605-1627	Reign of Jahangir, fourth Mughal Emperor
1612	Beginning of East India Company trade
1628-1658	Reign of Shah Jahan, fifth Mughal Emperor
1658-1707	Reign of Aurangzeb, sixth Mughal Emperor
1737	Nadir Shah of Persia invades Delhi
1757-1858	British East India Company rule
1837-1857	Reign of Bahadur Shah II (Zafar) last Emperor
1857	Indian Uprising
1858-1947	Crown rule in India (British Raj)
1947	Indian Independence

*****

WHO'S WHO AND WHAT'S WHAT

Abdul Hamid Lahori	Author of *Badsha-nama*
Anarkali	Rumoured to have been Prince Salim's lover
Ag Qoyunlu	'White Sheep' Turkomans
Aisan Daulat Begum	Grandmother of Babur
Akbar	Third Mughal Emperor
Andijan	Birthplace of Babur
Arghun	Ruling dynasty of Kabul
Aurangzeb	Sixth Mughal Emperor
Babur	First Mughal Emperor
Baburi	Young friend of Babur
Bahadur Shah II	Last Mughal Emperor
Bairam Khan	Commander of Mughal army, Regent to Akbar
Barlas	Tribe of Timur
Begter	Half-cousin of Genghis Khan
Beyzid I	Ottoman Sultan
Borijin	Tribe of Genghis Khan
Borte	Wife of Genghis Khan
Bulaki	Son of Krusau
Captain Hawkins	Companion of William Finch
Chagatai	Second son of Genghis Khan
Chand Bibi	Regent Queen of Ahmadnagar
Daniyal	Third surviving son of Akbar

Dara Shikoh	Eldest son of Shah J
Fakru	Son of Zafar
Farid Khan	Birth name of Sher Shah Suri
Fatawa-e-Alamgiri	Islamic Code commissioned by Aurangzeb
Francis Xavier (Jesuits)	Co-founder of Society of Jesus
Genghis Khan	Great Khan of the Mongols
Gulbadan Begum	Sister of Humayan, author of *Humayan-nama*
Guru Arjun Dev	Fifth Sikh Guru
Hanafi	Islamic Jurisprudence following Abu Hanifa
Hamida Banu Begum	Wife of Humayan and mother of Akbar
Hemu	Hindu General fighting for Afghan warlord
Hindal	Brother of Humayan
Hindavi Swarajya	Hindu self-rule
Hoelun	Mother of Genghis Khan
Humayan	Second Mughal Emperor
Ibrahim Lodi	Ruler of Delhi
Inyat Khan	Biographer of Shah Jahan
Islam Shah Suri	Second Emperor of the Sur Empire
Jamukha	Friend of Genghis Khan
Jawan Bakht	Son of Zafar, the last Emperor
Jemadar Prasad	Sepoy in Bengal Native Infantry
Jochi	Eldest son of Genghis Khan

Keraite	Turkic-Mongol tribe
Khanwar Battle 1527	Town near Agra, location of
Khalji	Dynasty ruling Delhi Sultanate
Khasar	Brother of Genghis Khan
Khongirad	Turkic-Mongol tribe
Khurram	Third son of Jahangir
Khusraw	First son of Jahangir
Kwarezmian Mamluk origin	Persian dynasty of Turkic-
Ladli Begum	Daughter of Nur Jahan
Maham Begum	Fourth wife of Babur
Maham Angar	Foster mother of Akbar
Mamluks founded by slaves	Islamic Empire in Egypt
Mumtaz Mahal Shah Jahan	Niece of Nur Jahan and wife of
Manbhawati Bai	First wife of Jahangir
Mangal Pandey	Sepoy in Bengal Native Infantry
Mansab troops	Rank measured in numbers of
Mariam-uz-Zamini	Hindu Rajput wife of Akbar
Merkits	Turkic-Mongol tribe
Muhammad Amin Kazwini	Author of *Shah-Jahan-Nama*
Muhammad Alam Shah	Son of Aurangzeb
Muhammad Azam Shah	Son of Aurangzeb
Muhammad-Hadi *Jahangirnama*	Author of Preface to
Mir Ali Shir Nava'i	Poet living in Heart

Mir Jaffa of Bengal	Commander-in-Chief to Nawab
Murad	Second surviving son of Akbar
Muzaffar Jung	Son of Nizam-ul-Mulk
Nadir Shah	Ruler of Persia
Naimans	Turkic-Mongol tribe
Naqshbandi	Islamic Sufi Order
Nasir Jung	Son of Ruler of Nizam-ul-Mulk
Nizam-ul-Mulk	Ruler of Hyderabad
Nur Jahan	Favourite wife of Jahangir
Ogedei	Third son of Genghis Khan
Padshah	King
Parviz	Second son of Jahangir
Pir Muhammad ibn Jahangir Timur	Grandson and successor to
Raja Bir Singh Deo	Assassinator of Abdul Fazl
Rana Sanga	Rajput ruler of Mewar
Rani Durgavati	Rajput Queen of Gondwara
Roshanara	Favourite sister of Aurangzeb
Ruqaiya Sultan Begum Consort	First wife of Akbar and Chief
Safavid	Persian Dynasty
Salim accession	Name of Jahangir before
Salima Sultan Begum	Chief wife of Akbar
Saray Mulk Khanum Timur	Chagatai princess and wife of
Sati	The self-immolation of widows

Shah Shuja	Second son of Shah Jahan
Shah Tahmasp	Safavid ruler of Persia
Shahryar	Fourth son of Jahangir
Shaikh Salim Chishti	Sufi Teacher
Sher Shah Suri (Sher Khan)	Afghan ruler of Bihar
Shivaji	Maratha King
Siraj Ud Daulah	Nawab of Bengal
Sultan Bahadur	Ruler of Gujarat
Tarabai	Regent Queen of the Marathas
Tatars	Mongol federation
Temujin	Birth name of Genghis Khan
Tengrism	Central Asian religion
Timur	Founder of Timurid Empire
Toghrul	Khan of the Keraite tribe
Tolui	Fourth son of Genghis Khan
William Finch	English trader with East India Company
Umar Sheikh Mirza	Ruler of Ferghana
Uyghurs	Turkic-Mongol tribe
Vasco da Gama	Portuguese explorer
Yesugei	Father of Genghis Khan
Zafar	Last Mughal Emperor
Zinat Mahal	Wife of Zafar

*****

WORKS REFERRED TO

Abraham Eraly, *the Mughal Throne,* Phoenix, 2003

Abu-l Fazl, *The Akbarnama,* Translation by H Beveridge, Asiatic Society

Alexander Kennedy, *Genghis Khan, the Flail of God,* Fritzenmedia

Gulbadan Begam, *The Humayun-Nama,* Translation by Annette Beveridge, Royal Asiatic Society, 1902

Jadunath Sarkar, *History of Aurangzib,* Sarkar & Sons, 1912

John Man, *Genghis Khan,* Bantam Books, 2004

Justin Marossi, *Tamerlane*, Harper, 2004

Pierre du Jarric S.J. *Akbar and the Jesuits,* Translation by C H Payne, Harper Brothers

The Embassy of Sir Thomas Roe to the Court of the Great Mogul 1615-1619, Edited by William Foster, The Hakluyt Society

The Jahangirnama, Translation by Wheeler M Thackston, OUP, 1999

William Dalrymple, *The Last Mughal,* Bloomsbury Press, 2006

*****

Printed in Great Britain
by Amazon